SHORT WALKS FROM

Dartmoor Pubs

Other areas covered in the Pub Walks series include:

Bedfordshire
Berkshire
Birmingham & Coventry
Bournemouth & Poole
Bristol & Bath
Buckinghamshire
Cambridgeshire
Cheshire
Chilterns
Cotswolds
Cotswold Way
County Durham
North & West Cumbria
South Cumbria
Dartmoor & South Devon
Derbyshire
Essex
West Essex
Exmoor & North Devon
Gloucestershire
Herefordshire
Hertfordshire
Icknield Way Path
Isle of Wight
Kent – the North Downs
Lancashire
Leicestershire & Rutland

Lincolnshire
North London
Middlesex & West London
Midshires Way
Norfolk
Northamptonshire
Nottinghamshire
Oxfordshire
Shropshire
South Downs
Staffordshire
Suffolk
Surrey
Surrey Hills
Thames Valley
North Wales
South Wales
Warwickshire
Wayfarer's Walk
Wiltshire
Worcestershire
Wye Valley & Forest of Dean
East Yorkshire
North Yorkshire
South Yorkshire
West Yorkshire

A complete catalogue is available from the publisher at
3 Catherine Road, Newbury, Berkshire.

SHORT WALKS FROM

Dartmoor Pubs

Michael Bennie

COUNTRYSIDE BOOKS
NEWBURY, BERKSHIRE

COUNTRYSIDE BOOKS
3 Catherine Road
Newbury, Berkshire

ISBN 1 85306 401 7

Designed by Mon Mohan
Cover illustration by Colin Doggett
Photographs and maps by the author

Produced through MRM Associates Ltd., Reading
Printed by Woolnough Bookbinding Ltd., Irthlingborough

Contents

Publisher's Note

We hope that you obtain considerable enjoyment from this book; great care has been taken in its preparation. However, changes of landlord and actual closures are sadly not uncommon. Likewise, although at the time of publication all routes followed public rights of way or permitted paths, diversion orders can be made and permissions withdrawn.

We cannot of course be held responsible for such diversion orders and any inaccuracies in the text which result from these or any other changes to the routes nor any damage which might result from walkers trespassing on private property. However, we are anxious that all details covering the walks and the pubs are kept up to date and would therefore welcome information from readers which would be relevant to future editions.

Introduction

The Dartmoor National Park is one of the most popular walking areas in Britain, and with good reason. The scenery ranges from wild, open moors and rugged tors to gentle streams, from rich farmland to beautiful wooded valleys. And in between are a whole host of unspoilt villages and hamlets, most with their own traditional pubs.

The aim of this book is to bring the two together: to combine beautiful and interesting walks which reflect the variety of the landscape with friendly, characterful pubs, with a sprinkling of interesting places to visit along the way. The pubs are all suitable for the whole family, as are the walks – they range in length from 1¾ to 4¾ miles. A few involve hills because that is the nature of the Dartmoor terrain, but the climbing is kept to a minimum and none of it is particularly strenuous.

Dartmoor has a lot to offer the visitor, and many of the walks take in places of special interest, ranging from prehistoric remains to a 20th-century abbey, from ancient wayside crosses to relics of the area's industrial past, from sites which provided the inspiration for literary works to those that have become associated with some of the myths and legends with which the moor abounds.

The pub commentaries are personal impressions, intended to give an idea of the atmosphere of the place, rather than detailed descriptions, but they do all give certain basic information: opening hours, the kind of food and drinks they offer, where children and dogs are allowed, etc. On the other hand, I have tried to make the route guides as comprehensive as possible, combining descriptions of the routes themselves with brief accounts of what you are likely to see along the way. These guides are supplemented by sketch maps, but if you would like more detail, you can refer to the Ordnance Survey maps indicated. The Outdoor Leisure and Pathfinder maps are more detailed than the Landranger series (1:25,000 as opposed to 1:50,000).

Finally, please respect the landscape of the National Park and the people who live and work there. The basic rules are simple: shut all gates, do not disturb farm animals, keep dogs under control (even

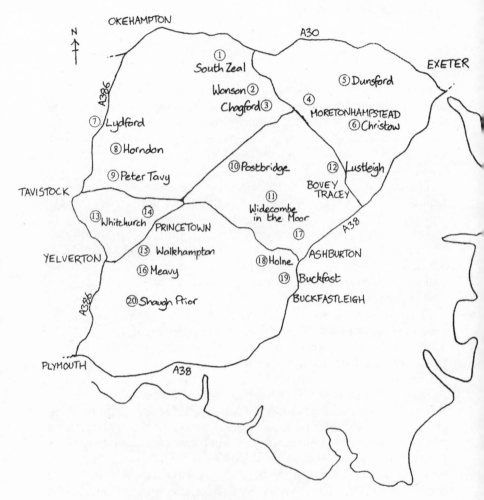

Area map showing locations of the walks.

on open moorland, where there may be sheep or nesting birds), do not pick wild flowers and do not leave litter.

I hope you get as much enjoyment out of this book as I did researching and writing it.

Happy walking!

Michael Bennie
Spring 1996

1 South Zeal
The Oxenham Arms

South Zeal is a picturesque old single-street village on the northern edge of Dartmoor, and the Oxenham Arms is very much in keeping with the village – one of the most charming old inns in the area. It is a granite building constructed by lay monks in the 12th century. It later passed into the hands of the Oxenham family, hence its name. The Oxenhams, whose line has now died out, suffered from visitations by the apparition of a white bird. If it was seen near a member of the family, he or she was about to die.

The inn has the old beams, stone walls and leaded windows one would expect in a building of that era, but it has more – a great deal of character. It comprises a cosy bar, partly panelled and with a beautiful granite fireplace, and a small family lounge, nicely furnished and with a monolith dating back some 5,000 years built into one of the walls. There is also a delightful dining room and a large garden laid to grass, with extensive views over the moors.

There are no fruit machines and no juke boxes (although there is a television in the family lounge) – it is just a superb family pub, full of atmosphere. Children are welcome in the family lounge and the

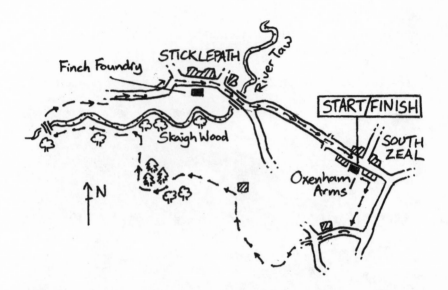

garden, and dogs are allowed. Accommodation is offered, and there is a separate (and very tastefully decorated) lounge for residents.

Opening hours are 11 am to 2.30 pm and 6 pm to 11 pm Mondays to Saturdays, and 12 noon to 2.30 pm and 7 pm to 10.30 pm on Sundays. Their traditional ales are Dartmoor Best and Jail Ale (which is brewed in Princetown, the home of Dartmoor Prison), and they also offer Tetley Bitter. Their draught lagers are Carlsberg and Kronenbourg and they have Inch's cider, Murphy's stout and Guinness on draught as well.

The food ranges from simple snacks to main meals like seafood parcels and their renowned steak, kidney, mushroom and Guinness pie. There is also an extensive vegetarian menu.

Telephone: 01837 840244.

How to get there: South Zeal is just south of the A30 Okehampton to Exeter road, and is clearly signposted from both directions. The Oxenham Arms is in the centre of the village. Several bus services pass the village.

Parking: There is a small forecourt in front of the inn, but this soon fills up, so it is better to park in the street, or in the public car park a couple of hundred yards down the main street to the east.

Length of the walk: 3 miles. Maps: OS Landranger 191 Okehampton & North Dartmoor area, Outdoor Leisure 28 Dartmoor (inn GR 651935).

The Taw River valley was made famous by Henry Williamson's classic Tarka the Otter, *and the stretch through Skaigh Wood is particularly beautiful. This route takes you up towards the moors, with one particularly good viewpoint, and then down to follow the river through the woods. You return to South Zeal via the attractive village of Sticklepath, where you can visit a water-powered forge dating back to the 19th century. There is a bit of a climb in the early stages, and a short scramble down to the river, but none of it is particularly difficult.*

The Walk

Turn right outside the pub, and follow the main street for a few yards until you come to a private drive leading off to the right with a chain across the entrance. There is no signpost, but inside the drive you will see a sign asking you to keep dogs on the lead. Go round into the yard behind the house to a gate, which leads into a field. Cross the field to another gate, and turn right into the road beyond.

When you come to the main road, go straight across onto a track (signposted 'Bridleway to moor') and follow it up the hill. Soon it curves to the right; at this point you should bear left, following the path sign, onto a short stretch of enclosed path. This soon rejoins the track, which then curves round to the right. At the top, go right (signposted to Ford Cross and A30), and at the gate to Beacon Cottage bear right onto a path between two walls.

The path ends at a track. Go right and follow the track as it winds down to a junction. Turn sharp left, towards the sign for Ford Farm. A few yards beyond this sign, the track forks. The signpost is not much help here, as both arms say 'Bridleway to moor', but you should take the right fork – which in fact means going straight on. It takes you through a gate and alongside a deep gully. Go through a second gate and then a third. Immediately after the third gate, turn right through yet another gate, following the bridlepath sign. There is a superb view from here right across the North Devon countryside, and it might be worth stopping and admiring it for a while, as this is the end of your climbing.

Follow the wall and fence on your right to the bottom of the field (do *not* take the more obvious track which leads off half left). Go through the gate on the right at the end, then left down into the woods, following the direction of the footpath sign. Keep more or less to the fence on your left, and ignoring the first stile you come to, go on down to the river. Turn left over the second stile and follow the riverbank through this delightful woodland, which is ablaze with rhododendrons in the spring and early summer.

This is *Tarka the Otter* country and on a sunny day, with the sun filtering through the trees and dappling the water, it is easy to picture him playing, hunting and fighting in the shallows. Sadly, however, you won't see any real otters.

After about 700 yards, you go through a gate and cross the river via a footbridge. The path curves round to the right and joins another one. Turn right onto this new path (signposted to Skaigh), which soon broadens into a track and leaves the river. You will come to a parking area and then a road. Go right at the road and past some houses to the main road. Turn right again into Sticklepath.

In the centre of the village, on the right, you will see Finch Foundry. Owned by the National Trust, it is a 19th-century forge, powered by a waterwheel. There are displays of tools and other artefacts, but the main attraction is the regular demonstrations that are held, showing the machinery at work. Behind the main building is a small garden and a tea room.

Carry on down the main street, and as you leave the village you will cross the river Taw again. Immediately after doing so, bear left down a side road, following the cycle sign. This will take you back to South Zeal. When you get there, go straight across the crossroads and you will soon find the Oxenham Arms on your right.

② Wonson
The Northmore Arms

This 400 year old pub just oozes atmosphere. It consists of two small, interlinked rooms, both with massive, bare stone walls and small windows, and both warmed by an open fire in winter. There is also a small beer garden. Children and dogs are welcome, and there is accommodation if you need it.

The inn lies on the Mariners' Way, an ancient route from North Devon to Dartmouth which was used by sailors changing ships, and it is said to be haunted by the ghost of an old bearded mariner – presumably one who didn't make it to his ship!

It is open from 11 am to 11 pm Mondays to Saturdays and 12 noon to 3 pm and 7 pm to 10.30 pm on Sundays, offering three traditional ales (Cotleigh Tawney, Dob's and Adnams Broadside) as well as Whitbread Best Bitter, Carlsberg and Stella Artois lagers, Murphy's stout and Dry Blackthorn cider. Food is on offer all day, and consists of good home-made staples like steak and kidney pie, sausage and chips, pasties, jacket potatoes and ploughman's lunches, with a roast on Sundays.

Telephone: 01647 231428.

How to get there: Wonson is a small hamlet between Throwleigh and Gidleigh. If you are approaching from the east follow the signs to Throwleigh from the A382 Moretonhampstead to Whiddon Down road. From the west, take the road to South Zeal from the A30, and then follow the signs to Throwleigh. Wonson is signposted from Throwleigh.

Parking: There is a small car park behind the pub, but it fills up very quickly, so your best bet is to park in the lane outside.

Length of the walk: 4¾ miles. Maps: OS Landranger 191 Okehampton & North Dartmoor area, Outdoor Leisure 28 Dartmoor (inn GR 674897).

This attractive – and for the most part relatively easy – walk follows quiet country lanes full of wild flowers down to the cool woods of Gidleigh Park (with the chance of seeing some deer) and the banks of the river Teign, and brings you back past a magnificent old manor house and through one of the most beautiful (and least known) hamlets in the area.

The Walk

Turn right from the pub, and follow the road up to the T-junction. Turn right (signposted to Forder, Chapple and Gidleigh) and follow the road as it winds past houses and a farm. Go straight on at the next junction and continue to follow the road signs to Chapple and Gidleigh. This is a very pretty lane, and as you go, you will catch occasional glimpses of Chagford Common in the distance.

Pass Chapple Farm, cross a stream and at the next junction go straight on (signposted to Gidleigh). After about ¼ mile, turn left (signposted to Gidleigh again). Very soon you come to Gidleigh church, which is worth a brief visit. There is a stream running through the churchyard, and stacked against the wall are a number of 17th-century tombstones. In the garden of the house next door are the ruins of a 14th-century castle. It is private property, but can be seen quite clearly from the gate.

At the next T-junction, turn right (signposted to Berrydown and Scorhill). There is a short climb for about 150 yards and then you will see a track leading off to the left (signposted 'Mariners' Way Teigncombe, Rd to Kestor Rock'). Take it, cross a stile and then

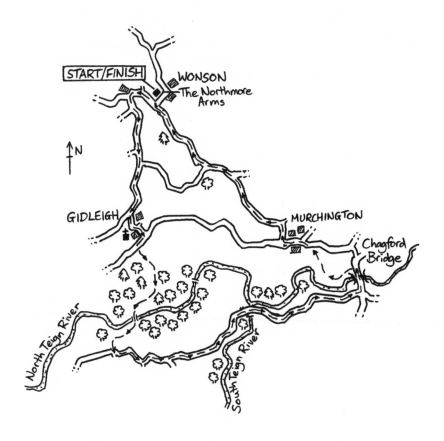

follow the track alongside a plantation. Go through a gateway and bear right and then left, following the 'path' sign to enter the trees.

The path takes you down through the trees, so tightly packed that no sky is visible and the path is bathed in an eerie half-light. At the end you join a track again and turn right (signposted 'public footpath'). You will see (and hear) the river Teign tumbling down on your left, and if you are quiet, you might just catch a glimpse of deer. After about 200 yards, turn left off the track to cross the river via a footbridge.

There is a fairly steep but short climb up the other side. At the top, turn right (signposted simply 'path') and follow the path round to the left to leave the wood via a stile. This brings you to a road, where you go left. Follow the road past Teigncombe Farm, with the open moors visible in the distance to the right.

After the farm, the road curves to the right and you will see an 'unsuitable for motors' sign on your left. Go straight on here rather than following the road round, down a narrow lane. As you pass the entrance to Northill on your left, the lane becomes little more than a wide path lined with walls and hedges.

At the end, when you join a road, go straight on. After about ½ mile, you will pass Holystreet Manor, a magnificent old house which dates back to the 15th century, although it has been extensively (and very well) enlarged this century. Admire it as you pass, but remember that it is private property and do not try to enter the gates.

At the next crossroads, turn left (signposted to Gidleigh and Throwleigh). Cross the bridge, and a short distance beyond it, turn left over a stile (signposted 'public footpath Murchington') to enter a wood. At the other end of the wood, go left, following the 'path' sign, cross a stream via some stepping stones and then cross a stile into a field. Go up the left-hand side of the field and cross another stile to a road. Turn left into Murchington.

Murchington is one of the prettiest hamlets in the area, with beautifully kept old farmhouses and cottages. Wander through it and at the junction on the other side, turn right. The road curves left and then right, and you get some very good views of the open moors ahead of you. At the T-junction, turn left (signposted to Providence, Wonson and Throwleigh). At the next junction, follow the main road round to the right (signposted to Providence, Wonson and Throwleigh again), and cross a stream. There follows the only long hill on the whole walk, but you can console yourself with the thought that you are nearly at the end. About ½ mile after crossing the stream, you will see a telephone box on your left. Turn right down the road opposite (signposted to Wonson and Throwleigh), and the pub is on your left.

Place of interest nearby
At Sticklepath, north of Throwleigh, is *Finch Foundry* a water-powered forge owned by the National Trust (see Walk 1).

3 Chagford
The Three Crowns

Chagford was one of the ancient stannary towns, where the tin miners of Dartmoor brought their tin to be assessed and weighed, and where transgressors against the stannary laws were tried.

The Three Crowns, in the centre of the town, is an extremely attractive two-star hotel, built of granite, and dates back to the 13th century, when it was a manor house belonging to the Whyddon (later Whiddon) family. This family is said to have inspired R.D. Blackmore's classic *Lorna Doone* – indeed, Mary Whiddon was shot dead by a jealous lover at the altar of Chagford church in 1641, in much the same way as Lorna in the novel.

The establishment's other claim to fame is that the poet and ardent Royalist Sidney Godolphin died here after being shot during the Civil War.

One enters through a beautiful stone porch, with the Godolphin bar on the left and the Whyddon bar on the right. Both have bare stone walls and magnificent granite fireplaces with open fires in winter. The Godolphin is the place for those who want entertainment: it has a juke box and television, plus a pool table and

darts board. The Whyddon has none of these, and is the place to go for a quiet, undisturbed drink. Both are pleasantly furnished and decorated. There is also a very attractive restaurant, a small lawn with tables at the back and a terrace of tables at the front, overlooking the street.

The bar hours are 11 am to 11 pm Mondays to Saturdays and 12 noon to 10.30 pm on Sundays, but they are happy for non-residents to join their guests for breakfast or coffee from 8 am. Both children and dogs are welcome.

On tap are Bass, Flowers Original and Flowers IPA, Heineken and Carlsberg Export lager, Guinness and Murphy's stout, Caffrey's Ale and Gaymer's and Addlestone's cider. The bar food ranges from ploughman's lunches and soup to fresh fish and chips (their speciality) and a very good steak and kidney pie. There is also

an extensive restaurant menu.
Telephone: 01647 433444.

How to get there: Turn west off the A382 Moretonhampstead to Okehampton road along the B3206, which leads straight to Chagford. There is a fairly regular bus service from Moretonhampstead and Exeter.

Parking: There is a car park to the rear of the hotel, but it is rather small and therefore reserved for residents. However, there is free parking in the street and in the public car park just up the road past the church.

Length of the walk: 3½ miles. Maps: OS Landranger 191 Okehampton & North Dartmoor area, Outdoor Leisure 28 Dartmoor (inn GR 701875).

Chagford is a pretty, vibrant little town, and this easy amble enables you to explore its beauty. It also takes you along the banks of the river Teign, through a delightful mixture of farm fields and woodland, with one or two quiet country lanes along the way.

The Walk

On leaving the pub, turn left into High Street. Follow it past the Square, with its attractive Market House on the right, into Mill Street and down the hill. Where the main road curves to the left, go straight on (signposted to Gidleigh and Throwleigh). This lane takes you out of town and down a steep hill. At the bottom, the lane levels off and you come to a crossroads. Turn right (signposted to Gidleigh and Throwleigh again).

You soon cross a narrow packhorse bridge. On the other side, turn right through a gate marked 'UTFA Private Fishing'. There is a public footpath sign, but you would be hard pressed to find it, as it is right in the middle of the hedge. You are now on the Two Moors Way, a long-distance path that stretches from the southern edge of Dartmoor to the northern edge of Exmoor.

Keep to the right of the field, alongside the river Teign to another gate. In the next field, you will see a row of oak trees which appear to be perched on stone platforms. They were, presumably, originally part of a hedge on top of a bank which was subsequently removed, leaving the oaks high and dry. The path follows them to a stile into the next field. It is very pretty along here, with the trees fringing the broad, gently flowing river on the right and farmland stretching away to the left.

You skirt two more fields before crossing a stile into a wood. Just beyond the stile is a weir. The river goes off to the right here, and the path follows the leat which leads off from the weir and flows on to Rushford Mill. You go through a gate and along the bottom of two fields. At the end of the second field, you cross a stile and a footbridge and go diagonally across the next field to a gap in the hedge, marked with a path sign. Cross the next field to a stile which leads you into a lane.

This is where you leave the Two Moors Way temporarily. Turn left up the lane, and follow it for about ¾ mile, passing the swimming pool, Rushford Mill Farm and Rushford Barton on your right and then Furlong Mill on your left. About 100 yards beyond Furlong Mill, you will see a footpath sign pointing to the right into a field.

Cross the stile and bear right across the field to cross a footbridge into a wood. Follow the path down through the wood to the river. It is a lovely stretch, and the ground is carpeted with pink purslane in the summer. When you reach the river, turn right (signposted to Rushford Mill and Chagford).

You are now back on the Two Moors Way. Make your way through the pretty wood, with the river cascading over the rocks on your left. You pass another weir and then leave the wood via a stile into a field. Keep to the left, alongside the river, and you will get a pleasant view across to Chagford Common ahead of you.

Cross another stile and keep to the left of the next field. This time, the view ahead is of Meldon Common, with Chagford Common to the right. At the end, turn right over a stile and cross a farmyard.

Turn left into the lane at the end. You pass the swimming pool again and then cross Rushford Bridge and climb gently to a T-junction, where the lane joins the B3206. Turn right and follow the road into the centre of Chagford. At the Square, turn left to the Three Crowns.

Place of interest nearby
Castle Drogo, an interesting National Trust house and garden, is a few miles west of Chagford, on the other side of the A382.

4 Moretonhampstead
The White Hart Hotel

Moretonhampstead is a good base for exploring north-eastern Dartmoor, and there is no better place from which to start your exploration than the White Hart. It is a 16th-century coaching inn, and during the Napoleonic Wars was a meeting place for French officer prisoners of war on parole from Dartmoor Prison.

There are two bars: a cosy public bar with a beamed ceiling, and an elegant lounge. There is also a beautifully furnished restaurant and a plain but very pleasant family room. Out at the back there is a courtyard in which you can sit in the sun. For those who want accommodation, there are some 20 rooms.

The food is excellent – all home-made and ranging from sandwiches, soups and local trout salad to their renowned steak and kidney and lamb, leek and apricot pies, with many vegetarian choices. Their traditional ales are Bass, Boddingtons and Poodle, and they have a wide variety of keg bitters, lagers and ciders on draught, as well as Guinness and Caffrey's Ale.

Both dogs and children are welcome, although dogs are excluded from the restaurant and children from the public bar. Opening hours are 11 am to 11 pm Mondays to Saturdays and 12 noon to

3 pm and 7 pm to10.30 pm on Sundays.
Telephone: 01647 440406.

How to get there: Moretonhampstead is at the junction of the A382 Bovey Tracey to Okehampton road and the B3212 from Princetown to Exeter. It is accessible by bus from all the main centres. The White Hart is right in the centre of the town, where the two roads cross.

Parking: There is a car park for residents across the A382 from the hotel. It is very small, however, and casual visitors would do better to park in the free public car park just a few yards further down the road.

Length of the walk: 3¼ miles (4¾ miles if you take the diversion to Cranbrook Castle). Maps: OS Landranger 191 Okehampton & North Dartmoor area, Outdoor Leisure 28 Dartmoor (inn GR 753860).

This is a very pleasant amble, mainly across farm meadows but with a bit of woodland and some good views to add variety. You pass the old almshouses on the way out, and if you are feeling energetic you can make a diversion to visit Cranbrook Castle, an Iron Age hill fort, from which the views are absolutely stunning. None of the walking is difficult, and what little climbing there is will not tax you.

The Walk
Turn right from the hotel entrance and cross the main road into Cross Street. You will see a large copper beech ahead of you on the left. This is called the Cross Tree and it was planted to replace an enormous elm, known as the Dancing Tree because dancing and other festivities took place on a platform built on its pollarded branches.

Just beyond the Cross Tree, also on the left, is a row of very attractive granite almshouses built in the reign of Charles I – you can clearly see the date 1637 carved above the main arch. Just beyond them, turn left through a kissing-gate into a children's play area. Keep to the left and you will come to a gate on your left leading into the churchyard. Go through it and turn immediately right

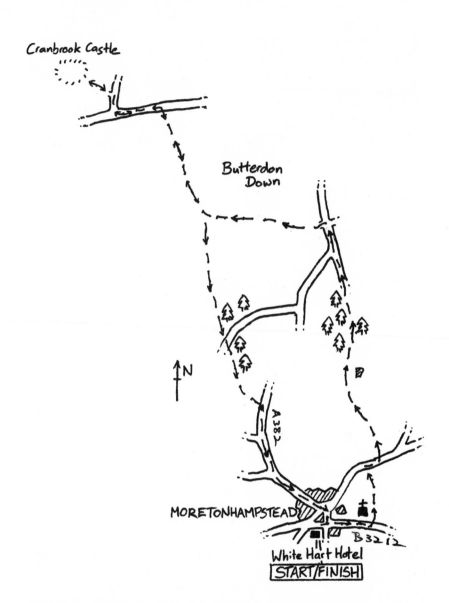

Cranbrook Castle

Butterdon Down

↑N

A382

MORETONHAMPSTEAD

B 3212

White Hart Hotel
START/FINISH

along a gravel path to a kissing-gate. Bear left down the field on the other side to another kissing-gate and onto a road.

Turn right and follow the road for about 100 yards until you come to a public footpath sign pointing left to the road near

The almhouses, Moretonhampstead

Butterdon. Cross a stile and go along the bottom of the field beyond, with a small stream on your left. Soon you go left to cross a stile and a footbridge and then right again to follow the opposite bank of the stream.

Cross another stile and keep to the bottom of the next field to a gap in the bank. Bear left here, following the direction of the path sign, and climb to the far left-hand corner of the field. Here you will find a stile. Cross it and turn left (signposted to the road near Butterdon Cottages). Cross another stile and keep to the right of the next field to yet another stile which takes you into some woodland.

The path leads you over another stile into an open patch and then back into the woods, meeting up with the stream again on your right. You soon go through a gate, however, and start climbing away from the stream, ending up on a broad grassy track. This leads to a stony track, where you should go right, following the public footpath sign. Soon you will get a good view to the right, across to Mardon Down.

Where the track meets a road, go straight on, and when the road curves to the right, turn left up a track (signposted 'Public bridlepath road near Bowden'). Don't go through the gate up ahead, but turn right between two walls to another gate, marked 'Public bridlepath'. Go through and turn left to skirt Butterdon Down. There is a magnificent view to the left from here, with Haytor on the horizon. At the end of the down, you have a choice: you can return direct to Moretonhampstead or make a detour to visit the Iron Age fortifications of Cranbrook Castle. The diversion adds about 1½ miles to the walk, but it is easy going and the views are outstanding.

To reach Cranbrook Castle, turn right at the fingerpost. At the next fingerpost go straight on (signposted to Cranbrook) and bear slightly right to another fingerpost. Cross three fields to a road and turn left. Follow the road for about 300 yards until you come to a track on the right. Turn right and after about 100 yards go left through a gate and up to the fortifications. They are quite impressive, especially on the southern side, where the massive banks and ditches are still largely intact. Climb to the top of the rampart for a view that will take your breath away – a glorious 360° panorama that takes in moors, farms and woods. Once you have had your fill, retrace your steps to Butterdon Down to rejoin the main walk.

If you decide not to visit Cranbrook, turn left at the end of Butterdon Down, and cross a stile. Cross four fields, keeping to the right all the time. There is a very good view ahead of you as you go. At the end of the fourth field, cross a stile to follow the edge of a conifer plantation.

Cross the road at the end of the path and continue across a stand of small conifers to a stile. Cross three fields, keeping to the right again. Go diagonally left across the fourth field and you will see Moretonhampstead in the valley ahead, with Haytor on the horizon. Cross a stile onto a road and turn right. At the junction with the main road turn left to return to Moretonhampstead. At the crossroads in the centre of the town, you will see the White Hart on your right.

Place of interest nearby
About 3 miles outside Moretonhampstead on the Princetown road is the *Miniature Pony Centre*.

⑤ Dunsford
The Royal Oak

Don't be misled by the exterior of this inn. Its Victorian red-brick design gives it a somewhat austere appearance, but inside it is warm, welcoming and very pleasantly decorated. One walks straight into a moderately sized bar, to the left of which is a delightful lounge area with an imposing fireplace containing a wood-burning stove. To the right is a light, airy non-smoking dining room and downstairs is a pool room. There is a courtyard beer garden at the back. It has the definite air of a village 'local', and is none the worse for that – visitors are made very welcome.

The food is all home-made, and there is a wide range available, from jacket potatoes to a variety of fish dishes and their speciality pies – mouthwatering offerings like steak, kidney and beer or lamb and mint. Accommodation is provided in converted barns at the back. Children are welcome, except in the bar itself, as are dogs.

There are always six cask-conditioned ales on offer, and they change regularly. In addition, they have Grey's and Scrumpy Jack cider, Heineken and Stella Artois lager, Guinness and Murphy's stout and an unusual offering – Hoegaarden wheat beer. Opening hours are as follows: Mondays, 12 noon to 2.30 pm and 7 pm to 11 pm; Tuesdays to Thursdays, 11.30 am to 2.30 pm and 6.30 pm to 11 pm; Fridays and Saturdays, 11.30 am to 3 pm and 6 pm to 11 pm; and Sundays, 12 noon to 3 pm and 7 pm to 10.30 pm.

Telephone: 01647 252256.

How to get there: Dunsford is just north of the B3212 Moreton-hampstead to Exeter road, and is clearly signposted from it. The summer Transmoor Link bus service calls there, and there are also services from Exeter and Moretonhampstead throughout the year. The Royal Oak is in the centre of the village, next to the church.

Parking: There is one pub car park across the road, and another behind the pub. The landlord has no objection to people leaving their cars there while walking, as long as they are customers of the pub.

Length of the walk: 1¾ miles. Maps: OS Landranger 191 Okehampton & North Dartmoor area, Pathfinder 1329 Topsham

Old water wheel at the iron mill

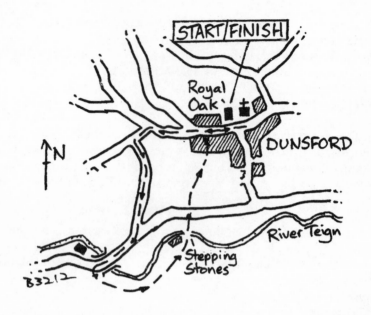

& Doddiscombsleigh (inn GR 812892). The middle of the walk can be found on OS Outdoor Leisure 28 Dartmoor, but Dunsford and its immediate surroundings lie just off it.

Bridford Wood is a beautiful National Trust nature reserve alongside the river Teign, noted for its wild flowers. We follow a quiet country lane down to it, wander through the trees to a delightful picnic spot by the river, and return to Dunsford across farm fields. The flowers in the wood are probably at their best in spring.

The Walk

Go past the pub car park, heading west out of the village. Pass the village sign, and turn left immediately afterwards. Follow the road round to the left (signposted to Steps Bridge and Moretonhampstead). It is a lovely lane, with an ever-changing assortment of wild flowers in the hedgerows on either side and a view of the woods covering the hillside ahead.

You pass a farm on the left and then go down to join the B3212, where you turn right. You will soon pass an iron mill on the left; notice the well-preserved waterwheel alongside it as you do so.

About ¼ mile after joining the B3212, you will cross the Teign via Steps Bridge. Follow the road round to the right on the other side until you come to the Steps Bridge Inn on the right. The view from here over the gardens and the river is lovely.

Immediately opposite the inn turn sharp left onto a path (signposted to Swannaford and stepping stones for Dunsford). This leads you into Bridford Wood. It is lovely mixed woodland, particularly attractive in the spring, when the wild flowers are at their best. The path is broad and grassy, and runs above the river, which is visible through the trees on the left. When the woods open out, the path divides; take the left fork.

This path takes you above and then round a house on the left until it meets a tarred lane at the gateway. Turn right onto the lane and then after about 50 yards go left onto another path (signposted 'Stepping stones for Dunsford'). Cross a field to the river. This is a lovely spot to stop for a picnic or a paddle on a hot day – it is green and shady, and the sunlight filtering through the trees makes highlights on the water flowing gently by.

Cross the river by the enormous stepping stones provided. Go to the right on the other side and then to the left, between two buildings, to reach the road. Do *not* take the path immediately opposite; instead, follow the road to the right for a few yards and take the next path on the left (signposted to Dunsford village). This takes you straight across a field and then alongside a hedge.

At the end of the field, go left across a stile and immediately right. You pass some trees and come to a short stretch of hedge on the left. Beyond this hedge, go half left to a stile. Follow the narrow path between a hedge and a fence to a small road. At the top of the road, turn right and go back past the car park to the Royal Oak.

Place of interest nearby
Castle Drogo, an interesting National Trust house and garden, is about 5 miles to the west, near Drewsteignton.

6 Christow
The Artichoke Inn

If you are looking for an unspoilt traditional Devon pub, you would have to go far to beat this one. Dating back to the 16th century, it is a pretty, thatched building comprising three interconnecting rooms, one of which serves as a restaurant, and outside is a courtyard with tables. There is a magnificent stone fireplace with an open fire in winter.

The food is home-made and ranges from bar snacks and sandwiches to tasty main meals such as rack of lamb, medallions of pork and red mullet. There is also an extensive vegetarian menu. The full menu is not available on Mondays, however – only snacks.

Their resident ales are Bass and Boddingtons, and there is a guest beer which changes regularly. They also have Whitbread Best keg bitter, Heineken and Heineken Premium lagers, Murphy's stout and Dry Blackthorn cider on tap. Opening hours are 11.30 am to 2.30 pm and 6.30 pm to 11 pm Mondays to Saturdays and 12 noon to 2.30 pm and 7 pm to 10.30 pm on Sundays. Children and dogs are welcome.

Telephone: 01647 252387.

How to get there: Christow is signposted from the B3193 Teign valley road, and is served by buses from Exeter and Newton Abbot.

Parking: The landlord has no objection to customers leaving their cars in the pub car park while they walk.

Length of the walk: 3¾ miles. Maps: OS Landranger 191 Okehampton & North Dartmoor area, Pathfinder 1329 Topsham & Doddiscombsleigh (inn GR 833849).

This is a lovely walk at any time, but it is at its best in late spring, when the rhododendrons are out, and in July or August, when the rosebay willowherb is in flower. It follows lanes and paths to the beautiful Kennick Reservoir and back, taking in a delightful woodland stretch along the way. It may be better to wear long trousers rather than shorts, as one or two of the paths are sometimes fringed with nettles.

The Walk

Turn right as you leave the Artichoke and then immediately left at the junction. After about 100 yards fork left for the climb up Dry Lane. As the road bends to the right, go left between two white houses (signposted 'public footpath'). Climb the steps and then follow a narrow path between two walls, with the hedge forming an arch overhead. At the end, go right to cross a stile.

Follow the direction of the footpath sign along the bottom of the field beyond, and then go up the right-hand side. Pause at the top for a good view between the trees on the right across the Teign valley. Keep to the right of the field to reach a stile leading into a lane. Turn left.

You will find yourself still climbing, but rather more gently this time, flanked by hedges, and with a patchwork of fields rolling away on either side. After about ½ mile the hedges give way to woodland on the right and open fields on the left. You will soon come to a junction, with the road to Bridford going off to the right and the main lane curving to the left. Go straight on, up a lane marked with a 'no through road' sign.

The hedges close in again and soon the lane deteriorates into a track. For a short distance the track is flanked by hedges of rhododendrons – a real picture in late spring. When the

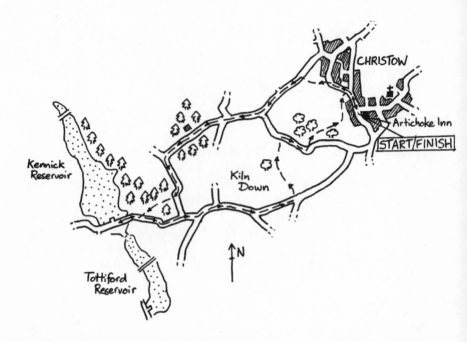

rhododendrons end, the terrain becomes more open and in July and August you will find the lane lined with a mass of pink rosebay willowherb. It enters a stretch of mixed woodland and then you will pass an old 17th and 18th-century Quaker burial ground on the right. There is nothing now to indicate its history except a plaque, but it has been taken over by rosebay willowherb. In season, it is a magnificent sight – a sea of pink rippling in the breeze.

At the T-junction by the corner of the burial ground, go left (signposted just 'bridlepath'). This track takes you through a conifer plantation, where every piece of open ground is again covered in rosebay willowherb in summer. The track turns to the right and then almost immediately to the left. Take the right turn, but where it turns left go straight on (signposted 'footpath'). Follow the broad, grassy track as it wanders in and out of woodland to a gate and stile leading onto a road. Cross the stile and go right to reach the dam wall of Kennick Reservoir. Kennick is one of three interlinked reservoirs, the other two being Tottiford and Trenchford. If you go onto the dam wall, you will see Tottiford Reservoir stretching away to your left.

The banks of the reservoirs are a mass of rhododendrons, and although the area attracts many visitors, most of them congregate around Trenchford Reservoir, where the main car park is. It is generally very peaceful up here and ideal for a quiet picnic, especially down towards the head of Tottiford Reservoir.

If you want to extend your walk at this stage, there are several paths around the reservoirs, and noticeboards to show you where they are. Our route, however, goes back along the road, the way we came down. Instead of crossing the stile back into the wood, however, keep to the road as it bears right. At the junction, go straight on (signposted to Christow and Ashton) and straight on again at the next junction (signposted to Christow).

At the next junction go left, down a lane marked 'unsuitable for motors'. After about ¼ mile, you will see a track going off to the right, but immediately opposite is a public footpath sign pointing across a stile. Cross the stile and go half left towards a gate on the other side of the field. Do not go through it, but turn right just

Kennick Resevoir

before, following the direction of the path sign. Keep the fence on your left, and follow the path as it goes in amongst some trees. You will come to a gate on the left, with a yellow dot on the gatepost. Go through it and turn right. Follow the fence (now on your right) for a short distance, until you come to another gate on the right. Go through it and then through a third gate on your left. This may seem complicated, but all the gates you need are marked with yellow dots, so it is actually quite easy to follow the route.

Cross a field to a fourth gate, also with a yellow dot on the post, and then follow a track round to the right to yet another gate and another track. Go straight on and then round the farm and through the gate straight ahead. The path on the other side leads down to a wood and then crosses a stream. Just before it does so, go left across a stile (signposted 'public footpath').

This new path takes you deep into the wood. You cross a wall by a ladder stile and then a fence by a step stile to enter a field. Go down the right-hand side of the field until you come to a gate on the right. Go through, cross the stream and turn left to follow it down through the trees.

You cross another ladder stile and then another step stile. Keep close to the stream to cross yet another step stile. The path now runs between the stream on the left and a fence on the right, with houses beyond the fence. It eventually comes out onto a road. Turn right to return to the pub.

Place of interest nearby
Canonteign Falls and Country Park are a few miles down the Teign valley road.

⑦ Lydford
The Castle Inn

This delightful freehouse is a fine example of a traditional Devon inn. Built in the 16th century, it oozes character. It comprises a small, low-beamed bar, a comfortable, well-furnished restaurant, a cosy snug, a large and attractive beer garden and a covered patio. The floors are of polished slate flags, the walls are decorated with prints and plates, and both the bar and the restaurant have open fires in winter. There is also an interesting collection of Saxon pennies minted in Lydford from AD 978 to 1050.

Opening hours are 11.30 am to 3 pm and 6 pm to 11 pm Mondays to Saturdays and 12 noon to 2.30 pm and 7 pm to 10.30 pm on Sundays. Dartmoor Best, Wadworth 6X and Palmers IPA are the regular real ales, with a guest beer that changes weekly, and they also offer draught Carlsberg and Stella Artois lagers, Inch's cider and Guinness. A wide range of wines is available by the glass.

The menu is impressive, ranging from tasty home-made steak and kidney pie to more exotic dishes such as Moroccan chicken. Their particular speciality, however, is Thai food.

Children are welcome, and dogs on leads are allowed in the bar

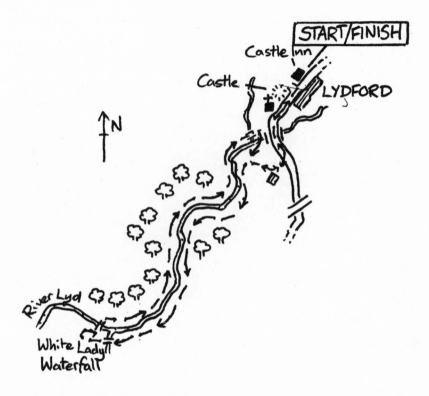

and on the patio. Accommodation is available.
Telephone: 01822 820241.

How to get there: Lydford is signposted from the A386 Tavistock to Okehampton road, and is well served by buses from Plymouth, Tavistock and Okehampton. The inn is towards the far end of the village.

Parking: There is a free public car park immediately opposite the pub, and it is probably best to use this if you are walking rather than take up space in the pub car park.

Length of the walk: 3½ miles. Maps: OS Landranger 191 Okehampton & North Dartmoor area, Outdoor Leisure 28 Dartmoor (inn GR 509848)

Lydford Gorge is a wonderland of rocks, woods and water, and this stunningly beautiful circuit takes you along the top of the ravine and back alongside the river Lyd. It is generally fairly easy and the path is very well marked, but there are one or two steeper sections – although even these are made less difficult by the provision of steps and handrails. On the way to the gorge, you can also explore Lydford Castle.

The gorge is a National Trust property, and there is a small entrance fee for non-members. Note too that this walk is only possible from 1 April to 31 October. For safety reasons there is access only from the southern entrance to the White Lady waterfall during the winter months.

The Walk

Turn right outside the pub, and you will almost immediately see the ruins of Lydford Castle on your right. It dates from 1195, and gained an infamous reputation as a prison, particularly for offenders against the stannary laws – those governing the tin miners of Dartmoor. Because prisoners were sometimes not brought before a judge for several years after being arrested, the notorious practice of 'Lydford Law' arose, under which offenders were hanged first and tried later! Entry to the castle is free.

Next to the castle is St Petrock's church, an attractive 15th-century building. If you visit it, look for the tomb of George Routleigh, watchmaker, close by the church wall, which has a delightful inscription on it.

Beyond the church, the road winds down and crosses the river Lyd. The drive up to the entrance to Lydford Gorge is on your right soon afterwards. Once in the National Trust property follow the path which leads down to a sign saying 'Way in'. The path zigzags down and then follows the side of the steep, narrow ravine, with the river Lyd occasionally visible below you on the right.

You will soon come to a T-junction. Turn left (signposted to the waterfall entrance) and follow the path as it winds away from the gorge, with a mass of wild flowers on either side. Go up some steps and you get a view of the river far below. The path winds away from the gorge again, climbing as it goes, but the going is made easier by more steps.

A little way beyond the bench at the top, you will cross a wooden footbridge and go up a few more steps. Then you start to

Lydford Castle

descend and cross another footbridge. After a short ascent up some steps, you begin to descend in earnest, again with steps to make the going easier.

The path levels off again and then climbs quite steeply (with steps again). Soon you turn right to cross a footbridge and then left up a gentle climb. At the top, go right to continue the walk (signposted to the White Lady waterfall). If you want refreshments or toilets you can go straight on (signposted 'Way out and refreshments'), retracing your steps to rejoin the circuit.

About 100 yards or so after the signpost, you have a choice of routes. You can go right for a shorter but steeper path down to the river, with steps and a handrail, or left along an easier path, but one which adds about 15 minutes to the walk. I would recommend the shorter route for anyone of average fitness, as it is not unduly steep, and the steps and handrail help.

The two paths come together again at the spectacular White Lady waterfall – an almost sheer drop of about 90 ft. It is a gorgeous spot, with the water cascading down and the sunlight sparkling on the river below. Local legend has it that if someone falls into the river here and sees a woman in white, they will not drown.

The path curves to the left below the waterfall, crosses a wooden footbridge and then goes right to follow the river Lyd upstream. Take care here as the path is rocky and can be slippery when wet. You climb up the side of the ravine for a short stretch (with steps), and then the path levels off. The river is still visible down on the right, with the sun dappling the surface as it filters through the trees.

The path soon rejoins the river and meanders alongside it. It is an idyllic stretch, with the river tumbling down beside you, the birds singing in the woods above you and wild flowers all around. You soon turn right on to a footbridge and join a wooden walkway with the river rushing down beside it in a series of stunning cascades.

Cross back to the other side and go through a short tunnel in the rock. It is very narrow in places, but there is a handrail to hold on to. Soon both the path and the river broaden out, and then you come to a footbridge on the right. Go straight on if you want to visit the Devil's Cauldron. At particularly busy times there can be up to an hour's wait to view the Cauldron itself, however, so if you want to bypass it, turn right over the footbridge for a short cut back to the entrance.

Otherwise keep on until the path turns right to cross a concrete footbridge and then goes left along the side of the gorge. You have to leave the main path for the short walk to the Devil's Cauldron, and only six people are allowed down at any one time. But it is an exciting sight as the water rushes through a narrow gap in the rock and boils around in the pool below.

Continue up the main path, and at the junction turn sharp right (signposted 'Way out'). At the top of this path is a picnic area, where you turn left for the exit. Go through the car park, down the drive and turn left at the road to return to the Castle Inn.

Horndon
The Elephant's Nest

Previously a row of 16th-century miners' cottages, the Elephant's Nest has been a pub for about 100 years. It gets its unusual name from a previous landlord, who was noted for his enormous size and who never seemed to move from his stool behind the bar. This prompted one of his regulars to comment that he looked like an elephant sitting on a nest, and the name stuck.

It is a lovely, old stone building, with a low beamed ceiling and a magnificent fireplace at one end of the main bar. At the other end are two interconnecting rooms, pleasantly furnished, for families, and there is a nice, sunny beer garden outside. Dogs are welcome.

There are always five traditional ales available: Boddingtons, Hicks and Palmers, plus two guest beers. In addition, they offer Heineken and Kronenbourg lager, Taunton Traditional cider, Guinness and Murphy's stout. The menu changes regularly, and ranges from ploughman's lunches and salads to exotic dishes like roast quail with sage and orange and vegetarian specialities such as ratatouille. The evening menu is more extensive than the midday one.

The pub is open from 11.30 am to 2.30 pm and 6.30 pm to 11 pm

Mondays to Saturdays and from 12 noon to 2.30 pm and 7 pm to 10.30 pm on Sundays.
Telephone: 01822 810273.

How to get there: Turn east off the A386 Tavistock to Okehampton road at Mary Tavy and follow the signposts for Horndon. The Elephant's Nest is on the right just before you get to the hamlet itself.

Parking: There is quite a large car park behind the pub, and the landlord has no objection to customers leaving their cars there while they walk.

Length of the walk: 3½ miles. Maps: OS Landranger 191 Okehampton & North Dartmoor area, Outdoor Leisure 28 Dartmoor (inn GR 517800).

Mining was one of the mainstays of the Dartmoor economy in days gone by, and there are many reminders of the industry still to be seen. We visit two very different ones – the Wheal Jewell Reservoir and the old engine house at Wheal Betsy – and take in a lovely stretch of moorland along the way.

The Walk
Follow the road on into Horndon and out the other side. Cross a cattle grid. At the top of the rise beyond the cattle grid, you get a good view of the open moor ahead and to the right. Soon you will come to a row of white cottages on the right. Turn left along the track which leads off immediately opposite them.

It is lovely up here. The low, curving horizon is broken by the odd tor, and the rest is just sky. It is also beautifully quiet and peaceful. You pass the pumping station for Wheal Jewell Reservoir on the right, and then the long narrow channel of the reservoir itself. It is fed by a leat, and this system once supplied three mines: Wheal Friendship, near Mary Tavy, Wheal Betsy, just across Kingsett Down, and Wheal Jewell itself. The reservoir is surprisingly well hidden – all that is visible from the track is the high bank which runs alongside it – but you can go across and follow it up if you so wish.

Near the end of the reservoir, you will come to a wall stretching

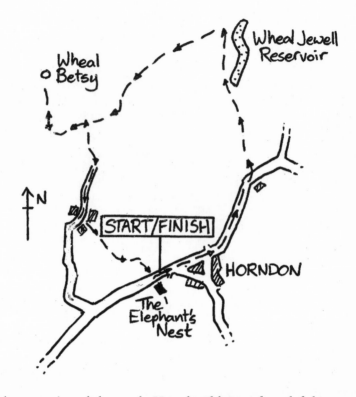

across between it and the track. You should turn *sharp* left here, *not* half left. As you do so, you will see a succession of stakes painted green at the top stretching across Kingsett Down. Follow them and soon the chimney of the Wheal Betsy engine house, and then the whole building, will be seen half right. There is also an excellent view across to Cornwall ahead of you.

Follow the stakes as they bear left, and you will find that they come to an end where a worn path comes down from the left. Turn right onto this path and follow it down to a gate with a bridlepath sign pointing through it. If you are worried that you might miss the turning (and this being open moorland, the paths are not always easy to see), then simply abandon the stakes when they bear left and make your way down to the fence you can see on the right. Turn left at the fence and follow it until you come to the gate and bridlepath sign.

Go through the gate and follow the track on the other side down across a field. It goes right at the bottom, through some gorse, and descends to another gate. Go through that onto a surfaced track and turn left to cross a stream. As the track curves left, turn right onto a broad path up to the Wheal Betsy engine house.

Wheal Betsy was a silver-lead mine which was reopened in 1806 and worked by water power until 1868, when this building was erected to house a steam engine. The mine finally closed in 1877, so the engine house did not have a very long working life. It is now owned by the National Trust.

To return, you should retrace your steps along the path to the track, across the stream, right through the gate on the other side and back up the field to the first gate you came through. Once through that gate, however, instead of going straight on, up Kingsett Down, turn immediately right along a track to a gate in the angle of the wall ahead. Go through it and follow the track down to a surfaced lane.

Where the lane bends to the right, turn sharp left into a farmyard (signposted to the Elephant's Nest). At the end of the farmyard, go right and then left, through two gates and into a field. Go diagonally across the field to a stile and a small wooden footbridge on the other side.

Bear left and go diagonally across the next field to the end of the wall ahead. Cross it via stone steps set into it, into the next, rather short, field and keep to the left. Cross the next wall and the fence beyond it via steps in the wall and a ladder stile. Keep to the left of the next field, also a short one, to another ladder stile. Climb it and go down the other side via steps set into the wall, then cross the stile in the fence immediately beyond. Go diagonally left to the corner of the next field to yet another wall with steps set into it. Cross this and keep to the left of the final field to reach the last wall of all, also with steps. Cross that into the road, and you will find yourself opposite the Elephant's Nest.

Peter Tavy
The Peter Tavy Inn

The Peter Tavy Inn is one of the many hostelries on Dartmoor that started life as church houses. It was built in 1480 to house the masons working on the church next door, and later became an inn to serve the packhorse men who passed by on their way across Dartmoor as well as the miners from the local tin mine. It is divided into three rooms, two of which have open fires. The slate floor, old beams and small windows give it a very distinctive charm, and if it is a sunny day you can sit in the grassed garden across the courtyard. Accommodation is also available.

They offer seven real ales which change regularly, plus Ansells keg bitter, Carlsberg and Carlsberg Export lager, Scrumpy Jack and Dry Blackthorn cider, and Guinness. The food is all home-made, and the menu ranges from sandwiches and rolls to venison, fish and the intriguing haggis supper. There is also a wide variety of vegetarian dishes.

Children are allowed in one of the rooms and in the garden, and dogs may be taken in as long as they are kept on the lead. The opening hours vary. From Monday to Thursday they are 11.30 am to 2.30 pm and 6.30 pm to 11 pm, on Friday and Saturday 11.30 am to 3 pm and 6.30 pm to 11 pm, and on Sunday 12 noon to 3 pm and 7 pm to 10.30 pm.

The landlord tells a delightful story about a churchwarden who was sent down by the vicar during Sunday services to make sure that no one was drinking at the pub when they should have been listening to his sermons. The warden, however, was related to the publican, so to avoid any problems he would walk slowly down the path with his eyes on the ground saying, 'I'm coming, Cousin Tom, I'm coming, Cousin Tom.' Needless to say, by the time he got to the pub all the drinkers had disappeared, and he could honestly report to the vicar that he had seen no one there!

A less respectable visitor was 'Axeman' Frank Mitchell, an associate of the Krays and the only man to escape from Dartmoor Prison and remain uncaptured, who used to drink there regularly during the 1960s.

Telephone: 01822 810348.

How to get there: Peter Tavy lies just east of the A386 Tavistock to Okehampton road, and is clearly signposted from there. The inn is at the end of the village, down a lane next to the church.

Parking: There is a car park behind the pub, and there is no objection to customers leaving their cars there while they walk, provided they ask permission first.

Length of the walk: 3 miles. Maps: OS Landranger 191 Okehampton & North Dartmoor area, Outdoor Leisure 28 Dartmoor (inn GR 512777).

This is a route for those who like a bit of variety in their walks. It includes rolling pastureland, riverside paths and a taste of the open moor. It is an undemanding ramble, with some quite outstanding views.

The Walk
Turn right down the lane running past the pub, and then right again up a track almost immediately beyond the entrance to the car park (signposted 'Bridlepath Mary Tavy'). There are banks of wild flowers on either side, and views across the farms to the moors

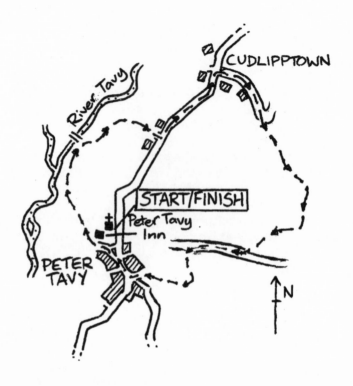

beyond. Where the track ends, carry straight on along a path. Soon you will hear and then see the river Tavy flowing gently by among the trees on the left.

Go through a gate and follow the path alongside a wall round to the right. Soon you will come to a wooden bridge across the river on your left. Do not cross, but go straight on (signposted 'Footpath county road'). This path takes you in amongst the trees along the river bank to a gate and stile. Go through and follow the path as it climbs away from the river, following an old pipeline.

Where the path forks, you can take either branch, as they join up again a few yards further on. Go through a gate into a field, and follow the broad, grassy track round to another gate in the fence on the right. Keep to the right of the next field, and you will have a lovely view across to the moors on your left. If you stop and look back, you can see Brent Tor, with its church perched right on the top.

At the top of the field, go through another gate onto the road and turn left. Follow the road for about ½ mile to the hamlet of Cudlipptown. At the junction in Cudlipptown, turn right, following a wooden sign for White Tor Stables. This road climbs past a farm and curves to the right, still climbing gently past more farm buildings. Where it bends very sharply to the left (almost back on itself), go right to cross a small stream. There is no signpost at this point, but soon after crossing the stream you will see one pointing to the moor.

Follow this path round to the left and you will be met with tremendous views to the right and behind you; on a clear day, you can see all the way to Bodmin Moor in Cornwall. Go through a gate and up a track. The tor on your left is White Tor. Follow the wall on the right to a gate, and keep to the right of the next field to another. Once through this gate, you will have the best view of the whole walk: a 180° panorama, with Great Mis Tor and Roos Tor on your left, Great Staple Tor and Cox Tor up ahead, and farms and villages stretching away to Cornwall on your right. The large rock formation immediately on your right is Boulters Tor.

About 100 yards beyond the gate, you will find a track. Turn right and follow it down to a road. Go right again, still descending quite steeply. Where the wall on the left turns sharply away from the road just before a group of houses, follow it round to a gate. There is a signpost at the gate pointing to the Combe, but none up at the road.

On the other side of the gate there is a path flanked by walls. It curves left round a house and down to another gate. Just beyond this gate, there is a junction where several paths meet. Turn right (signposted to Peter Tavy). Go through another gate and through some trees to a road, with the Colly brook keeping you company down to the left.

As the road turns left to cross the brook, notice the attractive old granite house on the right. Cross the brook and turn right to follow a path which runs along the bank for a short distance. It comes out at a road junction. Turn right and immediately right again. Just before the church turn left to return to the pub.

⑩ Postbridge
The East Dart Hotel

This 18th-century inn was originally a temperance hotel. It is now an attractive and popular pub, but still offers accommodation. It has a large bar, decorated with a frieze of hunting scenes, with a large stone fireplace enclosing a wood-burning stove. There is a carpeted lounge area beyond the bar, and a sunny beer garden at the back.

The light, airy restaurant, which is in the 'hotel' part of the inn, has a Sherlock Holmes theme (Sir Arthur Conan Doyle was a regular visitor to Dartmoor, and he derived much of the inspiration for *The Hound of the Baskervilles* from this area). It is decorated with Holmes artefacts and pictures.

The real ales are Dartmoor Best, Flowers IPA and Hicks Special Draught. Also on tap are Whitbread Best Bitter, Stella Artois and Carlsberg lager, Murphy's stout and Gaymer's Olde English Cyder. The bar food is all home-made, and ranges from pasties and rolls to more substantial meals such as steak and ale pie and lasagne. There is a separate restaurant menu.

Opening hours vary according to the season. In summer, the bar is open from 11 am to 11 pm Mondays to Saturdays and 12 noon to 10.30 pm on Sundays, although coffees and breakfasts are generally available from 9 am. Winter hours are 11 am to 2.30 pm and 7 pm to 11 pm Mondays to Saturdays and 12 noon to 3 pm and 7 pm to 10.30 pm on Sundays. Children are allowed in the lounge area, the beer garden and the restaurant, and dogs are welcome.

Telephone: 01822 880213.

How to get there: The inn is right on the B3212 Princetown to Moretonhampstead road. The summer Transmoor Link bus service passes the door, and there is a weekday service throughout the year from Tavistock via Princetown.

Parking: There is a car park alongside the inn, but it is small. It is probably best, therefore, to park in the large public car park a little further down the road towards Princetown.

Length of the walk: 3¾ miles. Maps: OS Landranger 191 Okehampton & North Dartmoor area, Outdoor Leisure 28 Dartmoor (inn GR 649789).

This is a delightfully varied route which takes in two lovely riverside stretches, some pretty forest walks, a taste of the moor and one outstanding viewpoint. It is fairly long but not at all strenuous.

The Walk

Make your way down to the bridge across the East Dart river about 100 yards or so from the pub. Go down the steps alongside the road bridge to reach the old clapper bridge just downstream from it. Cross it and turn left to follow the river (or linger a while to enjoy this lovely stretch of water). Soon you have to bear right to reach a gate in the fence ahead.

Go through the gate and climb to the open moorland above. Once you are out of the valley, start to bear right, aiming for the plantation you can see ahead of you. There is no clear path but the going is easy, and you get some good views to the left.

You will soon find the road on your right; you can walk along it or keep to the grass and walk parallel to it, depending on whether you prefer road or moorland walking. As you come over the crest of a small rise, you will see some white houses ahead. If you are

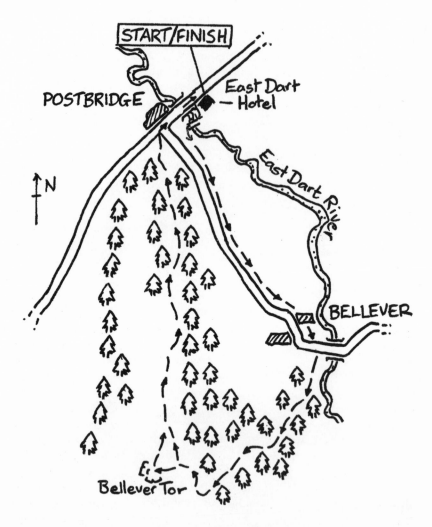

walking on the grass, aim to the right of them and pass them along the side of the road.

Where the road curves to the right, go straight on through a gate marked 'Bridlepath' and cross the stretch of grass ahead to the large, green Forestry Commission sign. Cross the road and make your way into Bellever Forest. The track takes you past a car park and some toilets on the right.

There is another lovely stretch of river on the left here, so if you want to stop for a picnic, go left just after the toilets. It is a marvellous place, with the forest behind you and the open moor in front, and children love playing in the water and on the rocks.

To continue the walk, rejoin the track and go right at the 'forest walk' sign. You pass through a picnic area and then through a gate. Go straight on up the track ahead, still following the 'forest walk' sign. At the top you will come to a cleared area, which is covered in gorse, foxgloves, rosebay willowherb and other wild flowers, depending on the season.

At the end of the cleared area, go right (signposted 'forest walk' again). Cross a stream and climb some steps. At the top is a T-junction. Go left (signposted to Bellever Tor). Follow the track alongside the trees, with another cleared area on the right, until you come to another T-junction. Turn sharp right. After about 200 yards go left off the track onto a rocky path marked with a red-circled post.

After a few yards, you have a choice. You can either bear left, following the sign to Bellever Tor, to climb the tor, or go straight on, following the red-circled posts alongside the edge of the plantation to bypass it. I would strongly recommend climbing Bellever Tor. It is not too strenuous an ascent, and the view from the top is magnificent – a 360° panorama. If you do climb it, bear right to rejoin the main route, following the broad grassy track which runs down to the long stretch of grass that divides the plantation almost in two, and make for the right-hand section.

Cross a broken-down wall and bear right into the forest again, still following the red-circled posts. You will soon come to another track. This is the Lichway, an ancient route with an interesting history. Until the 13th century, the Church insisted that people had to be buried in the churchyard of the parish in which they lived. This caused problems for the people of this area, because the whole of the old Dartmoor Forest, as far east as Bellever, falls within the parish of Lydford. So they had to carry their dead all the way across the moor to Lydford for burial, and the Lichway is the route that was used. This eastern section has not been used for that purpose since 1260, when Bishop Branscombe of Exeter allowed inhabitants of this area to use Widecombe Church, which is considerably closer, but most of the route can still be traced.

Cross the Lichway, following the sign for Postbridge. You go past a cleared area and then back among the trees. After a while the

The old clapper bridge, Postbridge

trees open out again and you get a beautiful view ahead. The track leads down to a gate. Go through it into a parking area and bear right to a road. Turn left and cross a cattle grid to reach the main road. Turn right to return to the pub or cross the road to the public car park.

11 Widecombe in the Moor
The Rugglestone Inn

Widecombe is one of the best known (and therefore most visited) villages in Devon, largely because of the song *Widecombe Fair*. The fair is still held every year, on the second Tuesday in September, and 'Uncle Tom Cobley' still makes his appearance there. It is an extremely pretty village which can become very busy during the summer, but most of the visitors are probably completely unaware of the unspoilt gem of a pub hidden down a side lane behind the church.

The Rugglestone is a stone-built inn which seems to have changed little during the 200-odd years of its existence. You will find no piped music, no fruit machines, no horse brasses here – just a simple but very attractive pub with a warm welcome and honest-to-goodness beer and food.

It comprises two small rooms, both with bare stone floors, beamed ceilings and warm log fires in the winter. There is also a lovely big garden with a stream running through it. For licensing reasons, children are restricted to the garden (which is probably where they would want to be anyway), but dogs are allowed.

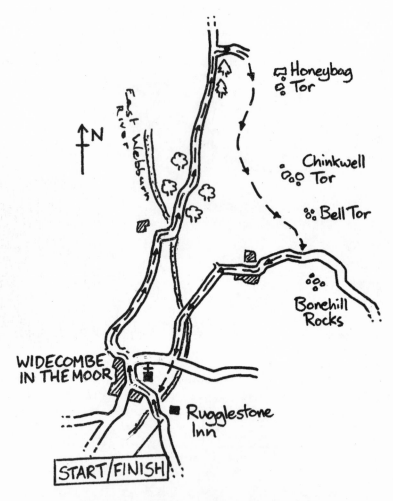

↑N

East Webburn River

Honeybag Tor

Chinkwell Tor

Bell Tor

Bonehill Rocks

WIDECOMBE IN THE MOOR

Rugglestone Inn

START/FINISH

The beer – Butcombe Bitter and Cotleigh Tawny – is served straight from the barrel, as is the local farm cider. Also on draught are Carlsberg lager and Murphy's stout. The food menu is not extensive – there are about ten different main courses on offer at any one time – but it is all freshly made and delicious. It is also very good value for money. Dishes range from simple ploughman's lunches to traditional favourites like steak and kidney pie, chicken pie and cottage pie.

Opening hours vary according to the day and the season. Midday hours are 11.30 am to 2.30 pm Mondays to Fridays, 11.30 am to 3 pm on Saturdays and 12 noon to 3 pm on Sundays. Monday to Saturday evening hours are 6 pm to 11 pm in summer and 7 pm to 11 pm in winter, and Sunday evening hours are 7 pm to 10.30 pm all year round.

Telephone: 01364 621327.

How to get there: Take the B3387 from Bovey Tracey, or leave the A38 at Ashburton and follow the signs for Widecombe. Follow the road round the church and take the first left to reach the Rugglestone Inn.

Parking: There is a large car park opposite the pub, and the landlord has no objection to customers leaving their cars there, as long as they ask permission.

Length of the walk: 3¾ miles. Maps: OS Landranger 191 Okehampton & North Dartmoor area, Outdoor Leisure 28 Dartmoor (inn GR 720765).

Quiet country lanes and rolling downs are the order of the day on this delightful ramble, with no strenuous climbs (unless you choose to scamper up one of the tors on the way). It also gives you an opportunity to explore Widecombe and its magnificent church, the setting for one of Dartmoor's most popular legends.

The Walk

Follow the lane back to Widecombe. As you approach the village, you will see the church, with the 120 ft tower which has earned it the nickname 'the cathedral of the moor', on your right. Also on your right, a bit further along, is Sexton's Cottage, an attractive 15th-century church house now owned by the National Trust.

Turn right at the T-junction to go into the attractive centre of the village, with its gift shops and cafés clustered around the village green. You will pass the church gate on your right. It is worth going in and exploring the light and airy 14th-century church, which has an interesting legend attached to it. There was a tinner of these parts called Jan Reynolds, who was said to have sold his soul to the Devil. One dark and stormy Sunday in 1638, he was sitting at the back of the church when there was a tremendous crash, and the Devil came

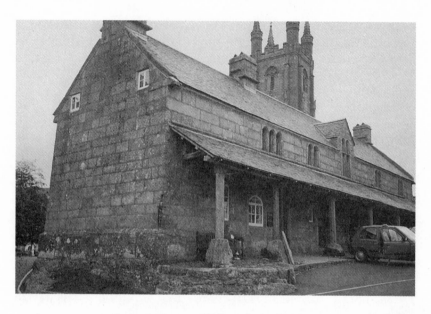

Sexton's Cottage, Widecombe in the Moor

through the roof and whisked him away to the top of the tower, where he had tethered his horse. As he rode off with the hapless Jan, his horse tore off the pinnacle to which it was tied, and it fell into the church.

Unfortunately, the historical account is somewhat more prosaic. There was indeed a violent storm on that particular day, but it was lightning which damaged the church, not the Devil and his horse.

Leaving the churchyard, turn right and then left (signposted to Natworthy). This lane takes you out of the village and past a tennis court. Soon it bends to the right and a number of tors appear just ahead of you: Honeybag, Chinkwell and Bell Tors, with Bonehill Rocks on the right. It is a pretty lane flanked by hedges.

After you pass Wooder Manor and Wooder Farm on the left, the lane turns right and then left to cross the East Webburn river and enter a stretch of woodland. It climbs gently and as you get to the top, a lovely scene appears ahead and to the left, of woodland, fields and moors. About ⅔ mile after crossing the river, you will come to a track leading off to the right just before a cattle grid. Turn up it and climb to a gate. Bear right beyond the gate and follow the track through the bracken along the foot of Honeybag Tor.

If you have the energy, you can climb up through the bracken and gorse to the top of the tor for some superb views – and children will also love playing on the rocks. Otherwise, keep to the track as it skirts round the base of Chinkwell Tor, with a good view down the valley to Widecombe and the farms of South Devon beyond. The track curves to the left round Bell Tor, and then to the right to join a road.

Just across the road and slightly to your left you will see Bonehill Rocks. If you did not have the energy to tackle Honeybag Tor, you might like to try the much easier climb here. Although the view is not as spectacular as from Honeybag Tor, it is quite extensive – and the rocks are almost as much fun for children to scramble over.

Turn right onto the road and follow it as it winds down the hill, past the pretty stone cottages of Bonehill and on to cross the East Webburn river again. After crossing the river, you pass a pretty wood on the right and then come to a T-junction. Turn left and almost immediately right across a stile marked with a public footpath sign. Keep to the left of the field beyond, alongside the river. At the far end, cross a low wall and a fence into a lane and turn left to return to the pub.

Place of interest nearby
The *Round House Craft Centre* at Buckland in the Moor has craft workshops, where one can see a variety of craftsmen at work, and a shop and restaurant.

12 Lustleigh
The Cleave

A cleave is the steep side of a valley, and this lovely, old, thatched inn derives its name from Lustleigh Cleave, a beautiful stretch of the Bovey valley to the west of the village of the same name, close to where this walk takes us.

Built in the 15th century, it lies in the heart of Lustleigh, among the attractive old cottages which cluster around the church. It comprises a small, cosy bar and a dining room at the front, with a family room and a larger bar, which is used mainly for overflow purposes, at the back. There is a vast inglenook fireplace in the front bar, and in the dining room the huge granite walls have been exposed. The place to be on a warm summer day, however, is in the garden, with its gorgeous display of plants and flowers.

The food is good and there is a wide choice, ranging from imaginative bar meals such as curries, steak and kidney pie, gammon and roast beef, to a full restaurant menu with separate selections for lunch and dinner. Their ales are Bass and Flowers Original, with a guest beer which changes regularly, and they also offer Whitbread Best, Guinness, Addlestone's cider and Heineken lager on draught.

They are open from 11 am to 3 pm and 6 pm to 11 pm Mondays to Fridays, 11 am to 11 pm on Saturdays and 12 noon to 10.30 pm on Sundays. Children are welcome in the garden and the family room, and dogs are allowed.

Telephone: 01647 277223.

How to get there: Follow the sign for Lustleigh leading west off the A382 Bovey Tracey to Moretonhampstead road. The village is served by buses from Newton Abbot and Moretonhampstead from Monday to Saturday.

Parking: The pub car park is very small, and it would be unfair for walkers to take up space in it when not actually using the pub, but you should be able to find parking alongside the road in the village.

Length of the walk: 2½ miles. Maps: OS Landranger 191 Okehampton & North Dartmoor area, Outdoor Leisure 28 Dartmoor (inn GR 785813).

Lustleigh is a delightful village of thatched cottages, as is the neighbouring hamlet of Pethybridge. This route visits both, and there is a lovely stretch through Hisley Wood in the beautiful Bovey valley. In fact, this is essentially a woodland walk, with just a bit of lane walking at the beginning and the end.

The Walk

Keeping the church on your right, go down to the Primrose Cottage tea rooms and turn left (signposted to Rudge). The old cottages and houses of the village have been well preserved, but this is no museum piece. It has a vibrant, 'lived-in' air which makes it one of the most attractive villages in Devon.

Keep to the main lane, ignoring the turnings to left and right, and as you leave the village you will begin to climb, first through trees and then through more open country. At the T-junction at the top of the hill, go left and then immediately right up the drive for Lower Hisley (signposted 'Public bridlepath Bovey valley and Hisley Bridge via Rudge Wood').

At the gate at the top of the drive, bear left onto a path between

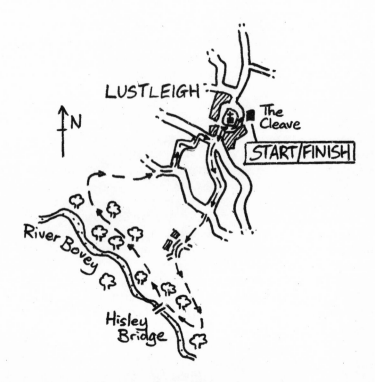

fences. Go through the gate at the end and turn right and then left through a stableyard. Go through another gate onto a path between high hedges, which leads you into a dense, dark wood.

The path descends gradually, then bends sharply to the right and the river becomes clearly audible down to your left. At the bottom, bear right, ignoring the track which goes sharp left. At the next junction, a few yards further on, however, you *can* turn sharp left for a detour of 100 yards or so to Hisley Bridge, a lovely, old packhorse bridge and an ideal place to stop for a picnic or for children to paddle or play in the river.

Otherwise bear right again, following the signpost to Lustleigh, along a broad track lined with wild flowers. At the first fork you can go either way, as the two tracks meet again after 50 yards or so, but at the next fork you should go right, following the yellow arrow.

Soon afterwards, you leave the mixed woodland and enter a conifer plantation. You also begin to climb. Where the track curves to the right, go straight on to cross a stile. Turn right and follow the path up through a mixture of rowan and hazel. The path is steep but mercifully short. At the T-junction at the top, go right (signposted to Lustleigh). When you come to a track, turn left and climb again to a gate which takes you out of the wood.

Beyond the gate, the track runs between hedges until it meets another one. Bear right here and follow the new track down between banks to join a lane. Turn right and after a few yards left into Pethybridge. You pass a very attractive thatched white house on the right. Immediately beyond it is a small lane marked 'unsuitable for wide vehicles'. Turn right here and follow the lane as it descends steeply past some more attractive houses.

It is a long and winding lane. After a while you will pass some Victorian terraced houses perched on the hillside on the left, after which the lane bends sharply to the right and then to the left. At the T-junction at the bottom, you should turn right, and at the next T-junction left. This is the road you came out on, so follow it back into Lustleigh and turn right at the church to return to the Cleave.

Places of interest nearby
The *Rare Breeds Farm* near Bovey Tracey, 4 miles to the south, is very popular with children. Also at Bovey Tracey is the *Riverside Centre*, the home of the Devon Guild of Craftsmen, with exhibitions and a craft shop.

⑬ Whitchurch
The Whitchurch Inn

Although Whitchurch is not strictly speaking on Dartmoor, the National Park is only a couple of hundred yards away, and most of this walk lies within its boundaries.

The Whitchurch Inn was built by monks in the 13th century as a church house, its function being to provide hospitality to travellers and those visiting the village church, which is right next to it. It also acted as an administrative centre for the church, and what is now the restaurant used to be the tithe room, where the locals paid their tithes to the Church.

It is a very small, cosy pub, with beautiful old oak beams, leaded windows and an open fire at one end. The delightful little restaurant is down a passage at the back. The pub is open from 11 am to 3 pm and 6 pm to 11 pm Mondays to Fridays, 11 am to 11 pm on Saturdays and bank holidays, and 12 noon to 3 pm and 7 pm to 10.30 pm on Sundays, and both children and dogs are welcome.

There are two regular real ales, Bass and Worthington, plus a guest beer which changes regularly. Also on draught are Worthington Best and Toby bitter, Worthington Mild, Tennents

Extra and Carling Black Label lager, Dry Blackthorn cider, Caffrey's Ale and Guinness. The food ranges from soups and pasties to curries, steaks and vegetarian dishes. Their traditional Sunday lunch is very good value, and they also offer a special OAP lunch on Thursdays.

Telephone: 01822 615383.

How to get there: Whitchurch is on the south-eastern outskirts of Tavistock, and is signposted both from the A386 Tavistock to Plymouth road and from Tavistock itself. The pub is in the centre of the village, just next to the church. The village is on the Tavistock to Plymouth bus route.

Parking: There is no pub car park, but it is generally fairly easy to find parking in the road. Visitors are asked to park carefully, however, so as to avoid obstructing the road or blocking any house or farm entrances.

Length of the walk: 3¾ miles. Maps: OS Landranger 191 Okehampton & North Dartmoor area (northern section of the walk) and 201 Plymouth & Launceston (southern section), Outdoor Leisure 28 Dartmoor (inn GR 493727).

Lush, green farms, cool woodland, rocky streams, gorgeous views and a taste of the wide open spaces of the moor – this lovely ramble has them all, and there are no steep climbs to contend with on the way.

The Walk

Turn left outside the pub and pass the church, which is worth a visit if you have the time. Immediately beyond the church you will find a kissing-gate on your right, with a public footpath sign. Go through the gate, but don't follow the direction of the sign, which points half right. Instead, go straight ahead, along the clearly marked path which follows the line of telegraph poles. This leads you across the field to another kissing-gate, on the other side of which it joins a road. After about 100 yards, this road joins another. Go straight on and then cut up left, off the road, along a track.

Where the track curves to the left, go straight on to a kissing-gate in the wall ahead. Keep to the right of the field on the other side to another kissing-gate, which leads into a cool, dark wood, with a

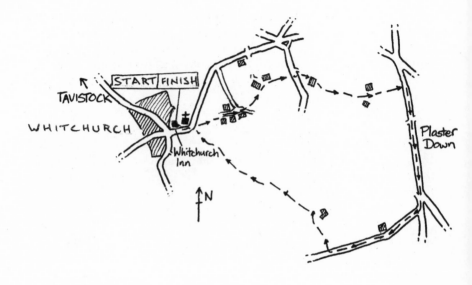

wooden fence and then a wall on the left. Go down some steps and turn left and then right, following the arrows. Cross a stile and keep to the left of the field beyond. At the end, you cross a wall via some stone steps set into it.

Keep to the left of the next field, with a typical Devon landscape of lush, green fields and trees stretching away on your right. Go through a gate and across the next field, still keeping to the left, then through another gate to a road. Turn left and then almost immediately right through a wooden gate marked with a yellow dot. This leads onto a drive.

Follow this drive round to the right. You pass a house on the left and go round another on the right. You will then find a small gate ahead. Go through it into another lovely stretch of woodland. After a few yards, the path forks. Go right, following the yellow arrow. At the end, cross a double stile into a field. Keep to the left and cross a stile at the end of the field into a driveway.

Cross to another stile immediately opposite and keep to the left of the next field. Go through a gap in the wall ahead and then bear left across the next field to a gate marked with a yellow circle. Go straight up the next field to another double stile, and straight across the next one, past an old corrugated iron shed to a ladder stile.

This leads onto Plaster Down, a gorse-covered stretch of open moorland. Follow the line of the wall on the right, and after about 100 yards you will get a magnificent panorama of Dartmoor. When the wall veers right, go straight on, picking your way through the gorse until you meet a road. You won't see the road until you are almost on it, but you can't miss it as it runs straight across the middle of the down.

It is beautiful out here, with the sky like a great vault above you and the moorland stretching away into the distance, and the only sounds are the bleating of the sheep and the song of the occasional lark. Turn right at the road, and follow it until it meets the wall on the right. About 50 yards after it meets the wall, there is a turning off to the right across a cattle grid, signposted to Fullamoor. Turn off here onto a pretty lane lined with hedges and a colourful array of hedgerow flowers.

After about ½ mile, you will see a footpath sign in the hedge on the right. Turn right across a stile (signposted to Whitchurch), and keep to the right of the field beyond. If you look to the left, you will be rewarded with a lovely view across the farmland of west Devon. Pass through a gate at the end of the field onto a track. Go right and after a few yards left (signposted 'Public footpath Whitchurch'). Pass through another gate and down the right-hand side of a field. Cross a stile and go on to the stream below.

Cross the stream, go through a gate and bear left, following the footpath sign to a metal stile. Go diagonally across the next field to a gap in the hedge, and across the next one to a stone stile. Cross the track on the other side and head for the stile on the far side of the field ahead.

Keep to the right of the next field, cross a stile, and again keep to the right to reach another stone stile. Bear left across the field beyond to a gap in the bank, and then go steeply down the side of the next field and through another gap to a stile and a footbridge across a stream. Make your way up the small hill in front of you, bearing slightly left, to the kissing-gate in the far corner of the field. This is where you started the walk, and you should turn left to return to the pub.

Places of interest nearby

Immediately north-west of Whitchurch lies the ancient market and stannary town of *Tavistock*. Of particular interest to children will be the *Meadowlands Leisure Pool*, with a variety of water attractions.

14 Princetown
The Plume of Feathers Inn

The Plume, as it is affectionately called, is truly an inn for all tastes. From breakfast to dinner, from a tent pitch to a four-poster bed, it offers a very wide range of food and accommodation, as well as a congenial atmosphere and a warm welcome.

Built in 1785, it is Princetown's oldest building, and its copper bars, log fires, slate floors and granite walls make it a delightful place to stop for a meal or a drink. In addition to two bars, there is a pleasant beer garden at the back and an enclosed adventure play area for children.

Whatever your accommodation requirements, they can be catered for. There are double and family rooms, two centrally heated bunkhouses with their own kitchens, showers and toilets, a 'stone tent' (a basic camping barn without its own facilities), and a large campsite. Breakfast is available from 8.30 am. The lunchtime and evening menu ranges from jacket potatoes, sandwiches and ploughman's lunches to steaks, chicken Kiev, curry and a variety of vegetarian meals. Their draught beers are Hicks Special Draught, Bass and Whitbread Best, and they also offer Toby Bitter, Whitbread

Dark Mild, Caffrey's Ale, Carling Black Label and Tennent's Extra lager and Taunton Traditional, Dry Blackthorn and Blackthorn Sweet cider.

The pub is open from 11 am to 11 pm Mondays to Saturdays and 12 noon to 3 pm and 7 pm to 10.30 pm on Sundays, and children and dogs are both welcome.

Telephone: 01822 890240.

How to get there: The pub is in the centre of Princetown on the B3212 Yelverton to Moretonhampstead road. There are bus services from Plymouth, Exeter, Tavistock and Newton Abbot.

Parking: There is a large car park to the rear of the pub, and the landlord has no objection to customers leaving their cars there while they walk.

Length of the walk: 3 miles. Maps: OS Landranger 191 Okehampton & North Dartmoor area, Outdoor Leisure 28 Dartmoor (inn GR 591735).

This interesting ramble enables you to enjoy the wide open spaces and magnificent panoramas of Dartmoor without too much effort, and to learn something of the history of the area. After visiting the fascinating Dartmoor exhibition at the High Moorland Visitor Centre, we follow the line of a disused railway to one of the old granite quarries and return across open country via one of the best viewpoints around Princetown.

The Walk

Cross the main road, and the building immediately on your left is the High Moorland Visitor Centre, which has exhibitions, displays and video and audio presentations which tell you about the geology, the wildlife, the history and the people of Dartmoor, and about the activities that take place there today. It is all extremely well presented, and a visit will help you to understand more about the area. What is more, it is free!

When you leave the centre, turn left and go round the building to the public car park. Follow the blue Tyrwhitt Trail signs across the car park, turning right in the middle to leave it via the vehicle entrance. Turn left, still following the three Tyrwhitt Trail signs.

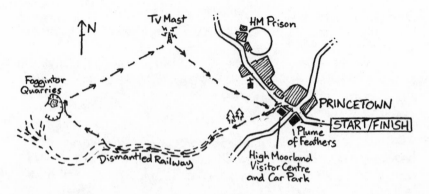

These trails are named after Sir Thomas Tyrwhitt, the founder of Princetown.

After a few yards, two of the trails branch off to the right. Keep straight on, following the sign bearing the train motif. A little further on a signpost marked 'disused railway' and carrying the motif, directs you half left to skirt some fields. It is a well-made path and you cannot miss the way. As you pass the stand of conifers on your right, the path broadens into a track. You are now following the route of Tyrwhitt's Plymouth and Dartmoor Railway. Built at the beginning of the 19th century, it was closed in 1956.

As you follow the dismantled railway, you will have a good view half left, over to Leather Tor and Sharpitor. About 1¼ miles after leaving Princetown, you will come to a stone bridge across a small stream. Cross it, and then turn right, making your way down the embankment and across to a path you can see bearing away from the main track. This area may be a bit tussocky and damp, but once you reach the path, you are on soft grass and the going is easy again.

Bear left along the path and follow it over a gentle rise. As you breast the rise, a superb panorama of the northern moors opens up ahead of you and immediately in front you will find an almost sheer drop into Foggintor Quarry, one of many disused granite quarries in the area.

Foggintor is an attractive place. The basin has filled with water to form a small lake, and it is a lovely spot to stop for a picnic. To reach the bottom, you need to skirt round to the right, where you will find an easy path down to the quarry entrance.

On leaving the quarry, turn right and aim for the television mast on North Hessary Tor. There is no clear path, but if you keep the mast ahead of you as you make your way through the tussocks of grass, you cannot go wrong.

It is a long but very gentle climb. As you go, notice the tall standing stone on your left. This is one of the markers of the ancient route across the moor from Tavistock to Ashburton. If you go up to it, you will see a T (for Tavistock) engraved on one side and an A (for Ashburton) on the other. This route was used before the road was built, and the stones ensured that travellers did not get lost in bad weather. A short distance further on, you will see another, similar stone on your right.

Aim to the right of the television mast. The views as you go are magnificent, and once you get to the top of the rise, it is worth pausing to take it all in. You will find a wall topped by a fence blocking your way up ahead. Turn right here to follow the wall down towards Princetown. To your left and ahead, the moors roll away beyond Princetown, while to your right you can see the tors above Burrator Reservoir again.

The path alongside the wall takes you down to a gate. Go through it onto a road. When the road bends to the left, you need to branch off onto a path. There is no footpath sign at the road, but there is one a few yards along the path. Follow the path to another road and turn left. Turn right into the car park, then left along the path back to the visitor centre and across the road to the Plume of Feathers.

Place of interest nearby
Princetown is renowned as the home of *Dartmoor Prison*. Although the prison itself is obviously not open to the public, there is a short trail which takes in some of the outer areas of the complex.

15 Walkhampton
The Walkhampton Inn

The plain white exterior of this 17th-century inn belies its character. Inside it is a charming, low-beamed granite pub, with three cosy, comfortable connecting rooms, the end one of which serves as a restaurant. It has a large collection of horse brasses (over 600) and some interesting hunting horns. At the back, there is a pleasant beer garden.

The atmosphere is very friendly, and both children and dogs are welcome. The cooking is superb, with a very varied menu provided by two live-in chefs. The food ranges from light meals such as soup and granary rolls to steaks, seafood specials, chicken Maryland and smoked cod pie. There is also an extensive vegetarian menu. Their speciality in summer is fresh sea bass.

The choice of beer is almost as wide as the choice of food. Their 'resident' traditional ale is Dartmoor Best, but they offer another six guest beers, which change regularly. Also on tap are Tetley's Bitter, Ind Coope Mild, Castlemaine, Carlsberg Export, Harvest Scrumpy and Guinness.

Winter opening hours are 11.30 am to 3 pm and 6 pm to 11 pm Mondays to Saturdays and 12.30 pm to 3 pm and 7 pm to 10.30 pm on Sundays. During the summer months, however, they are open all day (11.30 am to 11 pm) Monday to Saturday. They also offer bed and breakfast accommodation.

Telephone: 01822 855556.

How to get there: The village is a little way off the B3212 Yelverton to Princetown road, north-west of Dousland, and is signposted from there. There is a regular bus service from Yelverton, and a Sunday service from Plymouth.

Parking: There is a small car park in front of the pub, but this soon fills up, so it is better to park in one of the roads – it is not usually difficult to find somewhere.

Length of the walk: 2¼ miles. Maps: OS Landranger 201 Plymouth and Launceston, Outdoor Leisure 28 Dartmoor (inn GR 533696).

This is a short, undemanding ramble along farm paths and quiet country lanes. It passes through some beautiful countryside, with a number of stunning views.

The Walk

Turn right on leaving the pub, and follow the road for about 50 yards. Pause to admire Lady Modyford's School on the left. Founded by Lady Modyford in 1719, it is a charming granite building, and still houses the village primary school. Almost opposite the school, you will see a track signposted 'Footpath to road near Holwell via church'. Turn up here and go through a gate, soon followed by another one. Cross the field beyond, go through a gateway at the end and then across to a gap in the wall almost immediately ahead of you. There are extensive views from here, both to the left and to the right – it is rolling farmland for the most part, but there are a few tors in the distance on the left.

Bear right to cross the next field to a small kissing-gate in the wall ahead. This leads into a short stretch of woodland and round to the left-hand side of a churchyard. At the end of the path go right through another kissing-gate into the churchyard. Cross it and turn

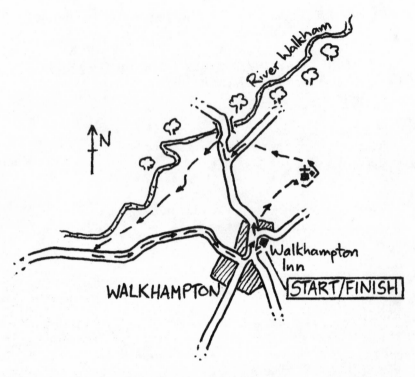

left to pass the church. It is an impressive building, and its tall tower is visible for miles around. Go through the kissing-gate at the end and turn left onto a track.

The house on your left is the Church House. Now divided into two cottages, it was originally the village inn, owned by the parishioners – indeed, it was an inn until the end of the 19th century. It also doubled as the village council chamber and a centre for the collection of tithes. Opposite the Church House is an old stone cross which was retrieved from a wall nearby and set up here. Where it was originally sited and what its purpose was remains something of a mystery, but it would most likely have been either part of a series of markers showing the route of one of the ancient ways across the moor or a preaching cross, beside which itinerant preachers would deliver their sermons.

Go straight on down the track (signposted to the road near Huckworthy) and through another kissing-gate alongside a cattle grid. Cross a stile and go down the left-hand side of the field

Wayside Cross, Walkhampton

beyond, looking out over another superb view as you go. Cross a stone stile and then a wooden one, and go down some stone steps onto a pretty path between two walls. There is a profusion of wild flowers along here, and birds of all kinds in the hedges alongside.

At the road at the bottom of the path, turn left. After about 100 yards you will come to a T-junction. Go right (signposted to Huckworthy Bridge and Woodtown), and after another 50 yards or so turn left onto a track (signposted 'Bridlepath Horrabridge'). The hedgerows on either side are still a mass of flowers, and the silence is usually broken only by the sounds of the birds and the occasional sheep.

Go through the gate at the end, and you will find a small stream immediately in front of you. Cross it via the stepping stones provided and bear left to meet a wall. Keep the wall on your right and you will soon join a broad track. Follow this track through the hawthorn and bracken for about ½ mile and you will come out at a road. Turn sharp left and follow the line of the road. It is unfenced on the left, so you can walk on the verge rather than the road itself if you prefer. The marvellous views open up again to the left and ahead, and there is a well-placed bench along the way if you want to sit and enjoy it for a while.

After about ½ mile, the road curves to the right and you are soon back in the village. At the T-junction, turn left to return to the pub.

Place of interest nearby
Burrator Reservoir, a beautiful picnic and recreational area which is very popular with families, is just a few miles away to the south-east.

16 Meavy
The Royal Oak

This is a friendly 14th-century inn which fronts onto the village green. It comprises two bars: a slate-floored public bar furnished with tables, stools and benches, and a carpeted lounge bar, furnished with padded chairs and settles. The lounge bar is perhaps the more comfortable, but the public bar has the advantage of a large open fire in winter. Both are full of character and atmosphere, with low beams and small leaded windows. Unfortunately, because both are served by the same bar, children are not allowed, but there are tables outside and the whole of the village green is at their disposal. Dogs are welcome.

The food is all good pub grub, and ranges from sandwiches to roast beef and a whole variety of vegetarian dishes, including a mouthwatering Stilton, potato and leek pie. They have an equally wide range of beverages on tap, including Courage Best, Bass, Otter and Royal Oak Strong in the way of real ales, three ciders – Scrumpy Jack, Taunton Traditional and Strongbow Extra Dry – Kronenbourg and Foster's lagers, Courage Mild and Guinness.

Opening hours are 11.30 am to 3.30 pm and 6.30 pm to 11 pm

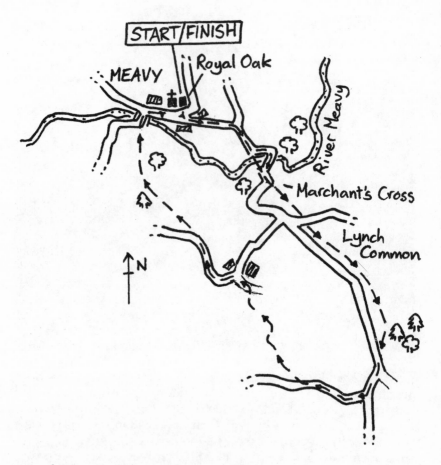

Mondays to Saturdays and 12 noon to 3 pm and 7 pm to 10.30 pm on Sundays.
Telephone: 01822 852944.

How to get there: Turn south off the B3212 Yelverton to Princetown road at Dousland. When you reach Meavy, turn right to the green and the pub.

Parking: There is a free public car park behind the parish hall across the green.

Length of the walk: 3¼ miles. Maps: OS Landranger 201

Plymouth & Launceston (start and finish), 202 Torbay & South Dartmoor area (central section); Outdoor Leisure 28 Dartmoor (inn GR 541672).

This very attractive ramble includes some lovely woodland and riverside stretches, magnificent views and a couple of interesting landmarks.

The Walk

Cross the green and turn left along the road out of the village. After about 400 yards, you will come to a T-junction. Turn right (signposted to Cadover). Where the road curves to the left, you can either go straight on to cross the river via some stepping stones and rejoin the road on the other side, or follow the road round in a loop to cross by the bridge. Children will probably prefer the stepping stones if the river is not too high, and the area around them is ideal for a picnic or a play in the water.

Go up the hill on the other side of the river, and cross a cattle grid. As the road curves to the right, you will see Marchant's Cross on your left. This is a very old cross; it was recorded as a boundary marker in 1280, but was probably erected some time before that. Travellers about to set off across the moor were said to kneel before it and pray for a safe journey in the days when crossing Dartmoor could be a perilous business.

Do not follow the road round, but go straight on, following the fence on your left. When the fence takes a sharp turn to the left, carry straight on up the hill among the gorse to Lynch Common. Pause at the top to admire the beautiful views to the north and east, with the great bulk of Sheeps Tor in the middle distance on your left.

You will soon see the road again on your right. You can either go across and join it or make your way through the low bracken more or less parallel to it. There is no clear path, but the going is fairly easy, as there are plenty of sheep tracks. If you choose the moorland route, you will soon cross a side road. Continue to follow the line of the main road, and the view opens up in front of you. You can now also see the wall of Burrator Reservoir over to the left. Aim for the plantation on the skyline ahead of you, and when you reach it turn right to rejoin the road.

At the first junction, follow the main route round to the right (signposted to Cadover Bridge). At the T-junction, go right (signposted to Clearbrook, Meavy and Yelverton). The road curves sharply to the right, and after about 500 yards you will see a track leading off to the right. Follow it through a gate.

There are more superb views ahead of you as you go down the track to another gate, which leads into a farmyard. Turn left in the farmyard and go through a third gate. Follow the track round to the right and then to the left between high hedges. After a short open stretch, you go through yet another gate, cross the Lovaton brook and go up to a tarred lane and some cottages.

Go left and left again at the T-junction, first down alongside the brook and then across it. About 150 yards after crossing the brook, look out for a stile on the right. There is no signpost, but the stile itself is marked 'footpath to Meavy'. Cross it and turn left. It goes through some trees for a short distance and then forks. The left fork goes up to an open field, while the right (more or less straight on) keeps to the woodland, following a wall. Take this right fork, and after a while you cross a stile.

This is a lovely, peaceful, shady stretch, with the Lovaton brook just audible over to the right. Cross another stile and go straight on (signposted to Meavy). Bear right at the end of the open field ahead to cross the brook once again and follow a track to yet another stile. This leads onto a wide path between walls, at the end of which is a gate leading onto the road.

Go right to cross a bridge, and at the T-junction turn right to return to Meavy. On your way back to the pub, have a look at the old oak tree at the end of the green. It is some 500 years old – some say it is even older, and was planted when the first church was consecrated, back in the 12th century – and has had to be supported, but it still seems to be flourishing. Another tradition has it that there was a preaching stone by the green, from which itinerant preachers used to give their sermons, and that the oak was planted to give shelter to their audiences.

Place of interest nearby
Just a few miles to the east of Meavy is *Burrator Reservoir* and a very popular walking, picnicking and recreational area.

17 Ashburton
The Victoria Inn

Ashburton is an ancient stannary town, where the miners of Dartmoor had to bring their tin to be weighed and stamped before it could be sold. It was also a centre of the wool industry, where wool from Dartmoor was spun and woven. Today it is an attractive and busy little shopping centre with a strong sense of history. It is an ideal centre for exploring south-eastern Dartmoor.

Originally a row of weavers' cottages, the Victoria Inn is a 500 year old stone building to the north of the town, backing onto the Ashburn river. There is one large bar inside, and a delightful little beer garden and children's play area across a footbridge at the back.

The pub offers a warm welcome and good home-made fare. If you only want a snack, there are pasties, ploughman's lunches and other light dishes to choose from. Those who want something more substantial might like to try their traditional favourites, such as steak and kidney pie and cottage pie.

Real ale enthusiasts can choose between Bass, Boddingtons and a guest ale which changes from time to time. Also on offer are Worthington Best bitter, Stella Artois and Heineken lagers, Dry

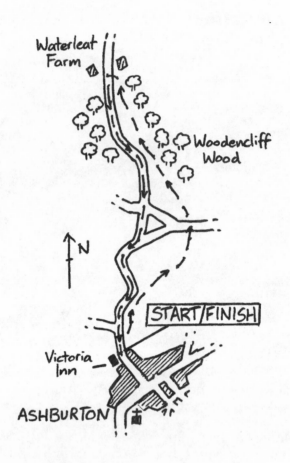

Blackthorn and Inch's cider, and Guinness and Murphy's stout.

Both children and dogs are welcome, and bed and breakfast accommodation is available. The pub is open from 11 am to 11 pm Mondays to Saturdays and from 12.30 pm to 3 pm and 7 pm to 10.30 pm on Sundays.

Telephone: 01364 652402.

How to get there: Ashburton lies just off the A38 Exeter to Plymouth road and is well signposted from both directions. There are regular bus services from Exeter, Plymouth and Newton Abbot. The Victoria Inn is at the top of North Street.

Parking: There is a large car park behind the pub, and customers may leave their cars there while they walk.

Length of the walk: 2¼ miles. Maps: OS Landranger 202 Torbay & South Dartmoor area, Outdoor Leisure 28 Dartmoor (inn GR 754701).

This is a walk for the wild flower enthusiast. It takes you across meadows, past hedgerows, through woods and along lanes, all of which offer their own floral delights. It is beautiful at any time, but particularly so in spring and early summer. The walking is very easy, with no climbing and no rough ground to negotiate.

The Walk

Turn left and follow North Street for about 50 yards until you come to a row of pink houses on the left. Immediately opposite them you will see some steps leading up from the road. There is a public footpath sign pointing up them to the Terrace Walk, but it is somewhat obscured, so you might miss it.

Go through a kissing-gate at the top of the steps and take the left-hand fork (signposted to Cuddyfoot Cross). The path, which is well used and easy to follow, runs initially along the bottom of the field, and then climbs slightly to pass above a barn. Cross the wooden stile in the fence ahead and then follow the path as it meanders alongside a stream at the bottom of the hill. This stream (the Ashburn) will be your cheerful companion off and on for much of the walk.

Cross a stone stile and, at the end of the next field, another. This brings you out onto a lane. Cross the lane to a public footpath sign pointing through a kissing-gate. Keep to the left of the field beyond and cross the wooden stile at the end. The path is now flanked by hedges full of wild flowers. The next stile takes you into a field, where you should bear right to enter the cool shade of Woodencliff Wood. You will have the woods on your right and meadows on your left.

A stile separates Woodencliff Wood from the next stretch of woodland, Whiddon Scrubbs. Immediately after the stile there is a choice of routes. A path goes off to the right, but you should ignore it and go straight on. These woods are renowned locally for their bluebells, and this stretch is quite delightful in spring, when they form a carpet of blue above you on the right. To add to the beauty of the scene, the river now reappears on your left, and the sunlight filtering through the trees dapples the surface.

At the next junction, go straight on again, following the river, and you will eventually come out onto a lane. Turn sharp left to cross a bridge, and follow the lane as it winds between hedges back towards Ashburton. There is little traffic and the hedgerows are home to a rich variety of flowers. About ¼ mile after joining the lane, look out for the strangely shaped Belford Mill on your left. As you approach, it looks rectangular, but if you look back when you have passed, you will see that it tapers almost to a point.

As you go down towards Ashburton, various lanes lead off to left and right. Ignore these and stay on the main road as it begins to descend. At the junction on the edge of town, go straight on and you will see the inn on your right.

Places of interest nearby
Ashburton has an interesting little local *museum*, and the *Chapel of St Lawrence* is worth a visit. Just outside the town on the Princetown road is the *River Dart Country Park*, with an adventure area for children.

18 Holne
The Church House Inn

Holne is a very attractive village, with some lovely cottages clustered around the pub, church and shop. The Church House Inn, as its name suggests, is next door to the church, right in the centre of the village. It is a 14th-century inn, built as a resting place for visiting clergy, and it still retains its traditional appearance and atmosphere, with low beams, leaded windows and timber partitions.

It comprises two small bars and a third room, the Kingsley Room (named after the author Charles Kingsley, whose father was vicar here), which serves as a lounge/family room. There is also a restaurant. The food is excellent – all home-made from fresh and, where possible, local and organic ingredients. There is a very good selection, ranging from ploughman's lunches and salads to a variety of hot main meals. Particular favourites are the venison in red wine and the rabbit pie.

Well-behaved children and dogs are welcome, and accommo-

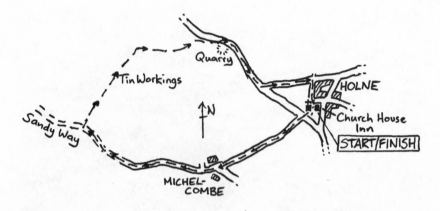

dation is available. They are open from 11.30 am to 3 pm and 6.30 pm to 11 pm Mondays to Saturdays and 12 noon to 3 pm and 7 pm to 10.30 pm on Sundays. They have a range of ales on tap, of which Dartmoor Best, Blackawton and Wadworth 6X are more or less constant, while the others tend to change from time to time. There is also Carlsberg Export lager, Flownes Neck cider and Murphy's stout on draught.

Telephone: 01364 631208.

How to get there: Holne is about 1½ miles from the Ashburton to Princetown road. The turn-off is about halfway between Holne Bridge and Newbridge, and is clearly signposted. At Holne, take the first turning into the village centre, and the Church House Inn is almost opposite you at the bottom of the hill.

Parking: Parking outside the pub is very limited, so walkers are recommended to use the free public car park about 35 yards down the road that runs to the left of the pub and church.

Length of the walk: 3 miles. Maps: OS Landranger 202 Torbay & South Dartmoor area, Outdoor Leisure 28 Dartmoor (inn GR 706695).

Holne Moor, which lies to the east of Holne, is a stretch of magnificent yet undemanding moorland with superb views on all sides. This walk enables you to experience the feeling of almost unlimited space and freedom that is such a feature of Dartmoor

without undue effort, and the routes to and from the moor take you
along pretty country lanes fringed with hedges and wild flowers.

The Walk

Turn left out of the pub and go round between it and the post office
to a gate into the churchyard. Go round the attractive medieval
church and across to a gap in the hedge, then half right to a kissing-
gate. Cross the field on the other side diagonally to a gate which
leads into a short path between two fences.

Go through the kissing-gate at the end of the path and cross the
road on the other side to a lane (signposted to Michelcombe). The
lane begins to descend, and you get a good view across to the moors
ahead. Continue for approximately ½ mile, enjoying the profusion
of wild flowers in the hedgerows on either side as you go, until you
reach the hamlet of Michelcombe. At the junction here, go straight
on (signposted 'No through road, bridleway only').

Go up the lane, and where it ends, carry straight on through a
gateway up the hill. (The route is signposted 'Bridlepath to the
moor', but only once you have passed through the gateway.) You

The view from Holne Moor

are now on a delightful shady track flanked by walls and banks topped with trees. There follows a long but fairly easy climb, and at the top you go through a gate onto the open moor.

Follow the broad grassy track which leads straight up ahead of you (*not* the rutted track which goes off to the left). This is part of Sandy Way, one of the ancient routes across the moor. After you have gone 100 yards or so, stop for a while and look around you, and you will appreciate the essential allure of Dartmoor. There are superb views to left, right and behind you, the stillness is almost tangible, and the sky is like a vast dome above you.

The track crosses a small stone bridge spanning Wheal Emma leat, now a dry channel but once a major water supply for the tin mines. Towards the top of the rise, you will come to another channel with a lone hawthorn by it. Turn right and follow it to a gully running down to the right. This part of the moor is covered in such gullies, which are usually all that remains of what was once a flourishing tin-mining industry.

Cross the gully and bear right, aiming for the corner of the wall you can see in the middle distance. When you reach it, take the path which follows the line of the wall but runs a little above it, still with panoramic views ahead and to the right. Where the wall turns sharp right, go straight on.

After a while you will come to a point where the dry Wheal Emma leat crosses a farm leat which is still functioning. Cross the new leat, and turn right along the track which runs alongside it. This track soon bears left away from the leat. Follow it, cross another leat and go down alongside a high wall on the right. Turn left along the track at the bottom, which takes you to a road.

Turn sharp right, cross a cattle grid and follow the road down the hill. At the junction, follow the main road round to the left (signposted to Holne). It is a pretty stretch of road, with summer flowers in profusion in the hedgerows and a small water channel flowing alongside on the right. About 500 yards beyond the junction, turn right (signposted to Holne village centre and Buckfastleigh), and return to the pub.

Place of interest nearby
Venford Reservoir, a popular place for family outings, is about 1½ miles north-west of Holne.

19 Buckfast
The Abbey Inn

The Abbey Inn is in an idyllic situation, right on the river Dart (on which it has fishing rights), just below Buckfast Abbey. It is a very attractive place, with beautifully panelled rooms decorated with prints, and a lovely terrace overlooking the river. Accommodation is available.

The pub is divided into three: a small bar at one end and two interconnecting rooms leading off from it, the first of which contains the food bar and is classified as a bar by the magistrates, so that children are not permitted. They are, however, allowed in the second room, furthest from the bar, which is just as pleasant, and on the terrace. An interesting feature is the enormous fireplace between the two rooms, which has openings into both of them. Dogs are welcome, but only in the bar and on the terrace.

The menu is interesting and wide-ranging, and you can choose from a variety of simple snacks such as cheese platters or opt for something richer and more filling, like venison steak or duck breast with black cherry and brandy sauce. Fresh fish is a speciality: customers can choose their own fish and have it cooked to order.

John Smith's Magnet is their regular ale, and they also have two guest beers on tap, as well as Foster's and Kronenbourg lager, Beamish stout and Dry Blackthorn cider. Opening hours are 11 am to 3 pm and 6 pm to 11 pm Mondays to Saturdays and 12 noon to 3 pm and 7 pm to 10.30 pm on Sundays.

Telephone: 01364 642343.

How to get there: Buckfast is a small village just off the A38 Plymouth to Exeter road, somewhat overshadowed by its sister town Buckfastleigh. To reach it, leave the A38 at Dart Bridge (signposted to Buckfastleigh if you are travelling south, to Buckfast if you are travelling north) and follow the signs for Buckfast. You will see the Abbey Inn on the right, some time before you reach Buckfast Abbey. Buckfastleigh is served by buses from Plymouth, Exeter, Newton Abbot and Totnes.

Parking: The landlord has no objection to customers leaving their cars in the pub car park for the duration of their walk, provided they ask permission first.

Length of the walk: 4 miles. Maps: OS Landranger 202 Torbay & South Dartmoor area, Outdoor Leisure 28 Dartmoor (inn GR 743668).

There is something for everyone in this walk: the magnificent Buckfast Abbey, famous for its bees and its tonic wine; the tomb of an evil squire, said to be still haunted by his hounds; and in between, pretty country lanes, farm paths and some delightful woodland. There are a few stiff climbs, but nothing someone of average fitness cannot manage.

The Walk

Follow the road on towards Buckfast. As you go, you will pass a spinning mill, with a viewing gallery from which you can see the mill in action, and then the mill shop, where you can buy its products. At the roundabout, go straight on under an arch to reach the Buckfast Abbey complex.

The abbey church is a magnificent building, erected by four monks over a period of 32 years, from 1906 to 1938, and well worth a visit. It is open to the public when not being used for services, and

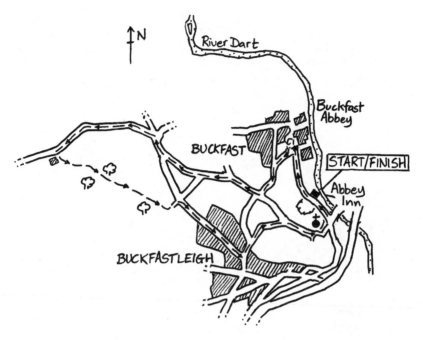

admission is free. In addition to the church, the complex contains a bookshop, a gift shop and a restaurant.

To return to the walk, go past the gift shop and follow the drive round to the left to the main gate. At the road, turn right (signposted to Holne). Climb past the turning to Buckfast itself, with a good view behind you over the abbey. At the crossroads at the top, turn right (signposted to Holne and Scorriton).

Follow this lane for a little more than ½ mile, ignoring the first three turnings (one to the right and two to the left) until you come to another crossroads. As you go, you will get a good view of the moors ahead of you. At the crossroads, turn left (signposted to Bowden and Cross Furzes). This lane takes you down between high hedges to cross the river Mardle and up the other side into a wood. It is a long climb, and steep initially, but it becomes easier after a while.

Towards the top of the hill, you leave the wood and come to Button Farm on your left. Turn left into the drive. There is no footpath sign at the road, but you will find one a few yards up the drive. Follow the drive round to the left and through a gate. Turn

Squire Cabell's tomb, Buckfastleigh churchyard

immediately right through another gate, with a yellow dot on the gatepost. Turn left and follow the fence along the left-hand side of a field.

In the far corner of the field, you will come to a stile leading into Bilberry Copse. Cross it and follow the path through the dense trees to another stile into a field. Keep to the right of this field to a third stile, to the right of the next field to a fourth and then to the right of the next field to pass behind a group of farm buildings to a gate onto a track.

Soon the track joins a surfaced lane. Where this lane joins another coming in from the right, turn left (there is a footpath sign, but it is hidden by the hedge). Go through a kissing-gate on the left, and keep to the right of the field beyond to a gate and a footbridge across the river Mardle again. Cross two stiles on the other side, to enter another stretch of woodland.

The path goes right and climbs through the trees. At the top, go sharp left, and then right at the fork, onto a broad path between two banks, which comes out at a lane. Turn right and follow the lane into Buckfastleigh. At the T-junction at the bottom of the hill, turn left into Church Street. Where the main road bears left, go straight on into Church Hill. Another climb follows, but it is rather more gentle than some of the others. At the top, follow the main route round to the right to reach the church – or what remains of it; it was gutted by fire in 1992. Go into the churchyard to visit the tomb of Squire Cabell, which is a large, square construction on the right of the path near the church door.

Squire Richard Cabell was a particularly evil man who was said to have sold his soul to the Devil. When he died in 1677, he was buried under an enormous stone slab, and this large building was erected around the tomb to keep him in his grave. He was a great huntsman, and it is said that on dark and stormy nights a pack of phantom hounds come howling around the tomb. He and his hounds served as the inspiration for Conan Doyle's famous Sherlock Holmes mystery, *The Hound of the Baskervilles*.

Carry straight on along the path through the churchyard to a gate and down some steps. At the bottom, turn sharp left and go down a steep and winding path between two walls. It comes out onto a track which leads down to a road. Turn left and return to the Abbey Inn.

Places of interest nearby
Buckfastleigh is the home of a *Butterfly Farm and Otter Sanctuary*, and it is also the start of the *South Devon Railway's* scenic steam journey down the Dart valley to Totnes. A few miles beyond Buckfastleigh is the *Pennywell Farm and Wildlife Centre*.

20 Shaugh Prior
The White Thorn

The White Thorn is somewhat deceptive; it is only 60 years old, yet it has all the atmosphere of a traditional Devon pub. This may have something to do with the beamed ceiling, the horse brasses and the open fire. It is a very good place to bring families in the summer, as there is a large adventure play area beyond the beer garden at the back, with a slide and a variety of other children's delights. Even in winter children are well catered for, with a pleasant family area at one end of the long bar. Dogs are also welcome, as long as they are kept 'on the lead and off the furniture' as the landlord puts it!

The food is mainly traditional pub grub, ranging from salads and ploughman's lunches (including a mackerel ploughman's) to seafood platter, chicken and chips and a range of interesting vegetarian dishes. The evening menu is more extensive, and includes a range of steaks, trout and salmon.

This is an Usher's house, and offers Usher's Best, Usher's Founder's and John Smith's on draught, as well as Carling Black

Label and Kronenbourg lager, Woodpecker, Strongbow Extra Dry and Scrumpy Jack cider, Guinness and Beamish stout. It is open from 11.30 am to 3 pm and 6.30 pm to 11 pm Mondays to Saturdays, and from 12 noon to 3 pm and 7 pm to 10.30 pm on Sundays. Telephone: 01752 839245.

How to get there: Turn east off the A386 Plymouth to Tavistock road just north of Plymouth and follow the signs to Shaugh Prior. The village can also be approached from the A38. Leave that road at Plympton and follow the signs to Lee Moor. At Lee Moor, turn left and follow the signs to Shaugh Prior. There is a fairly frequent bus service from Plymouth, which stops just outside the pub.

Parking: The landlord has no objection to customers leaving their cars in the car park while they walk, as long as they let him know.

The Dewerstone

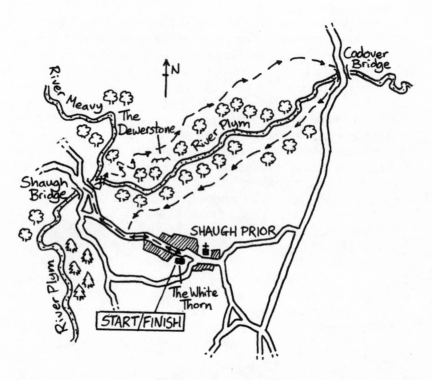

Length of the walk: 4¼ miles. Maps: OS Landranger 201 Plymouth & Launceston (start and finish), 202 Torbay & South Dartmoor area (central section); Outdoor Leisure 28 Dartmoor (inn GR 542631).

There are several Dartmoor legends concerning Old Dewer, the Devil. One is that he hunted across the moor with his pack of hounds at night, with humans as his quarry. The Plym valley is where the chase always ended, as Old Dewer drove his victims over the enormous rock known as the Dewerstone to their deaths below. This delightful route takes us to the scene of his dastardly deeds: into the beautiful Plym valley, through Dewerstone Wood and to the top of the Dewerstone. There then follows a stretch of moorland walking before we return on the other side of the river.

The Walk
On leaving the pub, turn left and follow the road past some modern

houses and out of the village. As you go, you get a pleasant view across woods and farms ahead of you. The road curves to the right and begins to descend fairly steeply. Ignore the side road going off to the left about halfway down; just keep straight on.

At the bottom, just before the bridge, turn right into a car park. Go through it, and follow a path round to the left to cross a wooden footbridge and go through a gate into Dewerstone Wood. This is a stunningly beautiful area, with the river rushing and cascading over the rocks, and it is very popular with families and picnickers.

Bear right after the gate, onto a path paved with granite. It soon climbs away from the river, running more or less parallel to it at first, but then climbing and winding away from it through the lovely broadleaved woodland. It is easy to follow, as it is the most obvious path for most of the way. It is only towards the top that you may become confused. Here you will find a path going straight on and another winding sharp right, almost back on itself. Take the latter. The paving soon ends and after a while you can see the top of the Dewerstone on your right. There are several rather gruesome tales of people plunging to their deaths from there accompanied by the sounds of hollow laughter, baying, thunder and vivid blue flames – the Devil obviously believed in giving his crimes the maximum publicity!

The path goes left, climbing steeply away from the river and the Dewerstone. After a short climb you leave the wood, cross a wall and climb up to the rocks ahead of you. This is the site of an Iron Age hill fort, and you will be rewarded for your exertions up the hill with superb views across Plymouth to Cornwall to the west, to the sea to the south and over rich, green farmland to the moors to the north.

Turn right and follow the path which runs through the bracken towards the edge of the wood and a group of rocks. Pass the rocks and go on until you reach a wall. Turn left and follow it round as it curves to the right. Soon a vast stretch of moorland comes into view beyond the china clay works which scar the landscape on the other side of the river.

The wall winds in and out, and there is no need to follow it exactly – just keep roughly to its line. You will pass a restored wayside cross, after which you should make your way down to the road and Cadover Bridge. It gets its name from the Celtic *cad*, meaning 'battle', and it is said that the sounds of fighting can still be heard from time to time, but what battle was fought here is not known.

Cross the bridge and turn right to go through the car park. Cross a stile to enter the wood, and after a short distance cross another stile. The path follows a disused – and now broken – pipeline, down which china clay was pumped, suspended in water, to a drying plant lower down the valley.

After a while, the path drops down a level via a small, one-sided ladder stile and you cross a wooden footbridge. The whole wood seems to have a green glow along here, as the rocks and tree-trunks are covered in moss and lush grass carpets the slope down to the river.

Cross a stile onto a bracken-covered hillside. You are now some way above the river, and another good view across Plymouth to Cornwall opens up. You can also see the Dewerstone and its associated rocks across the valley on your right. Still following the pipeline, the path re-enters the wood and starts to descend. Keep your eyes open as you go; you may be lucky enough to see a deer or two.

You soon come to a gate onto a track. Go through it (signposted simply 'path'), rather than bearing right to follow the sign to Shaugh Bridge, and turn right. Follow the track past some houses on the left, and at the bottom, where it joins the road, turn left to return to the village.

Place of interest nearby
The *Dartmoor Wildlife Park* at Sparkwell, about 6 miles south-east of Shaugh Prior, is very popular with children.